Hillstrom's Loyalty

Measuring Why It Is So Hard
To Grow a Business via Loyal Customers

Kevin Hillstrom

Acknowledgements

Thanks to all of the readers of my blog who questioned the logic of loyal buyer behavior and first-time buyer behavior. Their specific questions led to the creation of this booklet.

13 Digit ISBN: 978-1519244758+

Published in the United States of America by Kevin Hillstrom

Available from Amazon.com and other retailers.

Manufactured in the United States of America
First Edition

Cover Design: Kevin Hillstrom and Createspace.com
Cover Art: Kevin Hillstrom

Table of Contents

Surprise and Delight!

It is 2001. That's a long time ago! I am sitting in a conference room at Nordstrom, participating in a meeting with the loyalty team.

The room is full of ideas, bubbling with ideas, thoughts percolating at a rapid pace. A grease board smolders with residue from various markers.

Meeting attendees share ideas for how to increase customer loyalty at Nordstrom. A phrase is repeatedly used ... "*surprise and delight*". In my career, which at the time spanned thirteen years, I had not heard the term. The team wanted to identify ways to "*surprise and delight*" loyal customers. Random chocolates handed out to great customers. Free shipping. Concierge service. Advanced notice of trunk shows. The team wanted to spend money, but didn't have a lot of money. "*Would you be willing to fund free shipping?*" was a question fielded (the answer was no).

Not long after that meeting, the loyalty team disbanded.

While the team was disbanded, the concept of "*surprise and delight*" would stick with me for the next fourteen years! Why did the team members repeatedly bring up this topic? Did they know something that I didn't know? Was that the secret to keeping customers loyal?

Many of the employees participating on the loyalty team had worked previously at Starbucks. Their comments, thoughts/opinions, and tactics were offered at a rapid pace. Meanwhile, Nordstrom-centric employees in the meeting were largely quiet. This made little sense to me, because Nordstrom had the most loyal customers of any company I previously worked at. But it was the employees with Starbucks background that had the most to say.

A few years earlier, I worked at Eddie Bauer. We had a loyalty program. I measured the effectiveness of the program. Let me tell you, the program didn't exactly "push the peanut". I could not demonstrate that the program paid for itself. In other words, the discounts and promotions and points associated with the program cost money, and customers who took advantage of the free money did not spend enough incremental money to cover the cost of the program.

To summarize ... I had three data points ... an ineffective program at Eddie Bauer ... an unknown entity at Nordstrom ... and Nordstrom employees who previously worked at Starbucks and cared about loyalty with an almost religious fervor.

Who was right? Do loyalty programs pay off?

Good question!

A Meeting

A few weeks ago, I sat in a meeting. This company, like most of my client base, possessed a customer base with infrequent purchase activity. The average twelve-month buyer had about a one-in-three chance of purchasing again in the next twelve months. If the customer purchased, the customer would only purchase one or two times in the next year.

Executive leadership wanted to grow the business by *"getting customers to become more loyal"*. I pointed out that customers had comparable repurchase rates for the past five years, strongly suggesting that customers were never going to become more loyal. Executive leadership reminded me otherwise – they strongly believed that there was a secret formula that they had yet to crack, and once that formula was cracked, customers would immediately become loyal, and profit would fall out of the sky.

It was after that meeting, as I sat on an airplane, that I realized what the disconnect was. I recalled the meeting at Nordstrom, where Starbucks-centric employees loudly advocated loyalty initiatives. I thought about the meeting a few hours earlier, where the company possessed few loyal customers. What was the difference between the two companies?

Think about Starbucks for a moment. An existing customer has a 90% chance of purchasing again on a monthly basis, and if the customer purchases, the customer is likely to purchase several times per week. Meanwhile, the company I visited possessed a customer base where the customer had a one in three chance of buying again in the next year (not the next month), and if the customer purchased again, the customer purchased one or two times in the next year (not the next month). This disconnect doesn't happen because Starbucks is fundamentally better at fostering loyalty. Instead, the disconnect happens because of "frequency of want". The Starbucks customer wants to buy the product several times per week.

Now, let's be honest. Loyalty is a squishy concept. You might only buy a new car once every five years, but if you always buy a Toyota, you are loyal to Toyota. Meanwhile, you may not think much of McDonalds, but they are conveniently located and they serve food quickly and you are in a hurry, so you buy from them frequently. Or you like diet cola – so you purchase a Diet Coke if one is available, or you purchase a Diet Pepsi if one is available. To Coke and Pepsi, you are a loyal shopper, even though you are not loyal to either brand.

The purpose of this booklet, then, is to avoid arguing about loyalty – let the folks on Twitter argue without facts. My goal is to share facts. Based on the facts, you can decide for yourself whether you think your customer base will ever be loyal, whether a subset of your customer base is loyal, and whether you can implement a program that increases customer loyalty.

Facts

Loyalty initiatives have the potential to work when customers shop frequently. A frequent flier program has the potential to work because customers fly often enough to enjoy the rewards of the program. A frequent flier program is useless to a customer who flies four times per year. In fact, the loyalty program may have the opposite effect in situations where moderate fliers are faced with the challenges of a loyalty program. What is the point of a loyalty program if you are forced to sit in seat 64E, if you are forced to board in Seating Group 29, or if your luggage is tagged for free and delivered to Baggage Carousel 11? Why sit and watch the dozen members of the Elite Rewards program sit in first class sipping on wine? If you fly once a year, sure, you'll put up with it. But if you are in the middle of the pack, and not able to achieve Elite status, well, the whole system stinks, and you'll shop elsewhere based on price, convenience, and schedule.

You have to have a large number of loyal customers to offset any of the negative issues associated with a loyalty program. The large number of loyal customers have to deliver a ton of profit from loyalty initiatives to offset any associated negatives.

Think about it this way. Your customer base has to shop often in order to obtain benefits that pay for themselves and meaningfully grow the business. Look at the two customers below:

Customer #1 = 35% chance of buying again, 2 purchases per repurchaser.

Customer #2 = 80% chance of buying again, 10 purchases per repurchaser.

Customer #1 can be expected to place 0.35*2 = 0.70 purchases next year.

Customer #2 can be expected to place 0.80*10 = 8.00 purchases next year.

Let's pretend that you are a marketing wizard. Let's pretend that you have a secret up your sleeve, a secret so powerful that you can increase purchases per year by 10%. That's a big number, folks! It is really hard to encourage a customer to purchase 10% more often. If we assume you are a loyalty marketing genius, then what impact do you have on each customer?

Customer #1 = 0.70 purchases per year * 0.10 loyalty gain = 0.07 incremental purchases.

Customer #2 = 8.00 purchases per year * 0.10 loyalty gain = 0.80 incremental purchases.

Already, we can clearly see the facts surrounding loyalty programs. *Loyalty programs have no chance to move the needle when the customer has a low annual repurchase rate, or when the customer is unlikely to purchase more than a half-dozen times per year.*

Conversely, loyalty programs have the *potential* to move the needle when the customer is highly likely to purchase again, or when the customer is likely to purchase more than a half-dozen times per year.

A Rule of Thumb

When I evaluate businesses, I use a rule of thumb to determine if a customer (or brand) has a loyal customer base.

Here we go: *"If a customer or a segment of customers have a 60% chance of buying again in the next twelve months, then the customer or segment of customers is deemed 'loyal'"*.

Oh, I know, I know. You are not going to like that definition. *"You aren't including purchase frequency"*. *"A loyal customer is almost guaranteed to purchase in the next year"*. *"What about money, what about a customer who buys once every three years and spends ten thousand dollars each time?"*

If you don't like the definition, create your own definition!

Here's what I learned. Purchase frequency and annual repurchase rates are highly correlated. Run the analytics for yourself, you'll observe the same thing. As a result, I can greatly simplify all of the geeky wonkery required to think about customer loyalty by looking at just one metric. If I can demonstrate that a customer has a sixty percent chance of buying again in the next year, then I can demonstrate that the customer is highly likely to purchase 3 or 6 or 10 in the next year, and then, I can demonstrate the potential of a loyalty program.

So that's the definition I am going with. It will become obvious as we walk through the booklet that the vast majority of customers have no chance of becoming loyal, and that our view of customer loyalty needs to adjust.

The Customer Journey

One of the injustices of the digital era is that we can measure just about anything, but because we can measure just about anything, we seldom measure anything on a long-term basis.

Think about it. You can measure a search campaign down to the keyword, determining the series of keywords that are most likely to generate profit. You can measure whether a visitor from Pinterest is likely to purchase or not. You can follow a customer all across the internet, thrusting retargeting efforts in her face until she relents, measuring each and every interaction.

There are hundreds of thousands of analysts who know how customers respond to campaign-centric activities. These are smart people, no doubt about it! But if you ask 100,000 analysts how many first-time buyers purchase for a second time within a year, well, you'll be lucky if 5% of the analysts can answer the question. Heck, you'll be lucky if 1% of the analysts can answer the question.

And therein lies the problem.

The customer journey is a long, plodding process that almost never results in a loyal shopper. For the vast majority of businesses we work for, the customer journey ends following a first purchase.

Did that sentence sink in?

Let me repeat the sentence.

"For the vast majority of businesses we work for, the customer journey ends following a first purchase."

Here's a graph for a typical e-commerce business. In the graph, I measure the probability of a customer purchasing for a second time, given that the customer has not repurchased after "x" months.

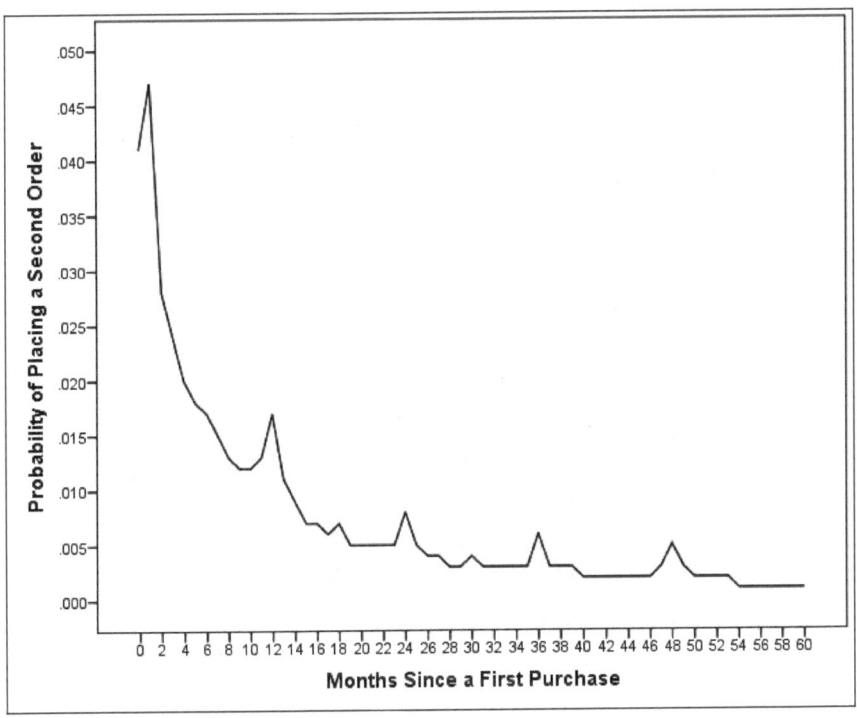

Months Since a First Purchase

Tell me what you observe?

First, the customer is reasonably likely to purchase for a second time in the three months following a first purchase. But after the first three months, the customer slowly goes dormant.

Second, there are blips in response ... at month twelve, month twenty-four, month thirty-six, and month forty-eight. These are seasonal trends. In these cases, the customer purchased, say, in November, and then purchases again the following November, or two Novembers later, or three Novembers later ... you get the picture, right?

Here's another way to view the information. Instead of looking at the conditional probability of a second purchase, let's look at the cumulative probability of a second purchase by time. Here we go!

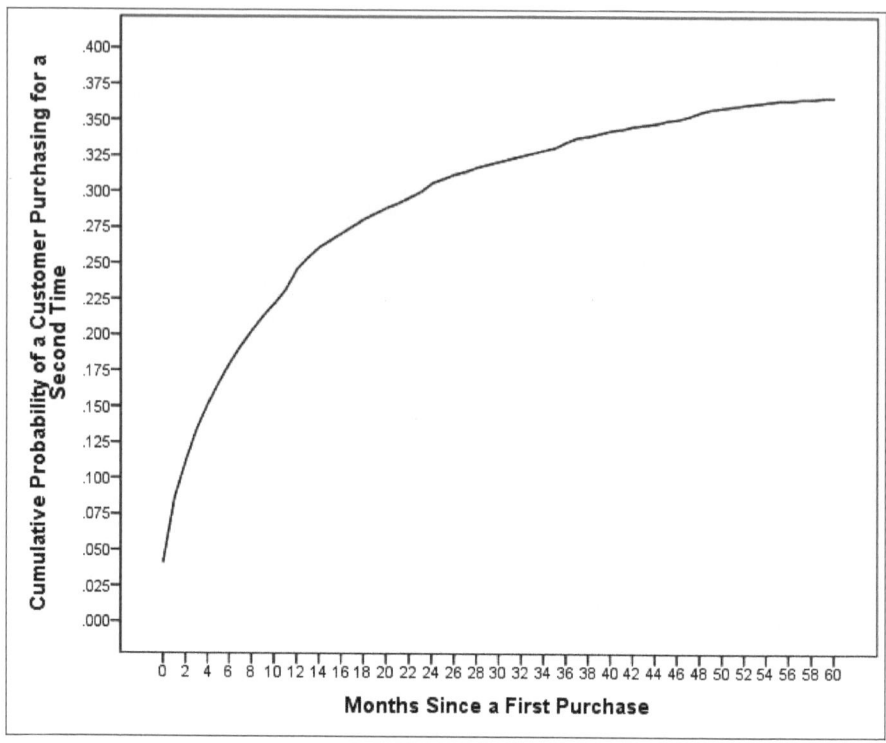

Oh oh.

After five years ... *five years* ... only 36.6% of first-time buyers have purchased for a second time (in this example – a typical example). That's fewer than 3 in 8 first-time buyers repurchasing again in five years.

This is such an important point, folks. This is what e-commerce repurchase metrics usually look like. There are a ton of customers who purchase, and those customers have no interest in purchasing for a second time. If the customer has no interest in purchasing for a second time, why do we think we can cause the customer to become loyal?

There's a reality we have to face. The vast majority of customers we manage are customers with few purchases, and with very little interest in purchasing again. If we can manage this relationship profitably, then it is fine to encourage customers to buy again. But if we cannot manage this relationship profitably, then we are better off letting the customer go, finding a new customer instead.

At this point, you are probably wondering what happens when a customer purchases for a second time, right? Does the customer become loyal after a second purchase?

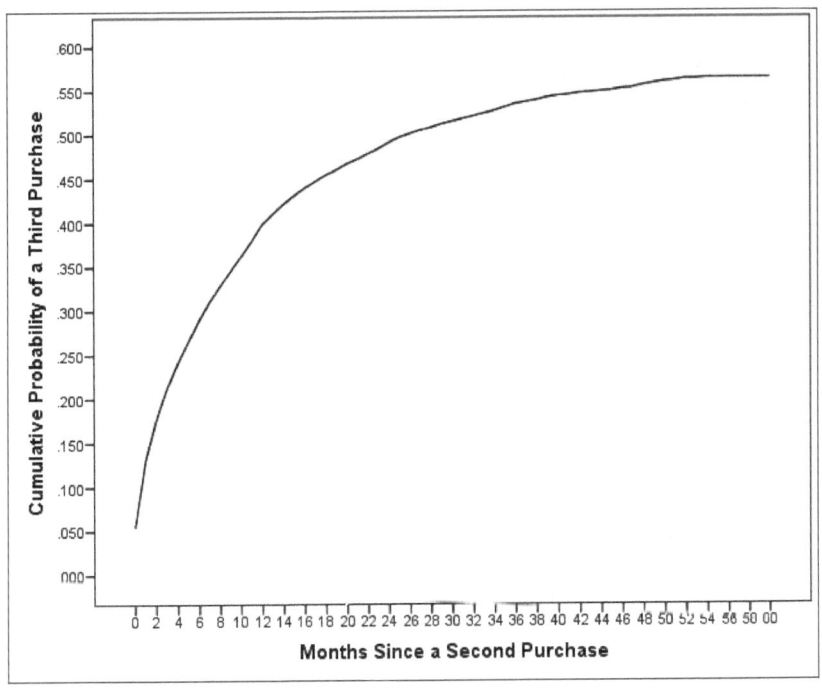

Well, the story looks better, but the story still isn't great. After twelve months, the customer has a 40% chance of purchasing for a third time. After sixty months, five full years, the customer shopping this brand has a 56% chance of purchasing for a third time.

Remember, my definition of a "loyal" customer is a customer who has a 60% chance of purchasing again in the next twelve months. Clearly, a customer who purchased for the second time has yet to achieve "loyal" status.

What does the graph look like for third-time buyers?

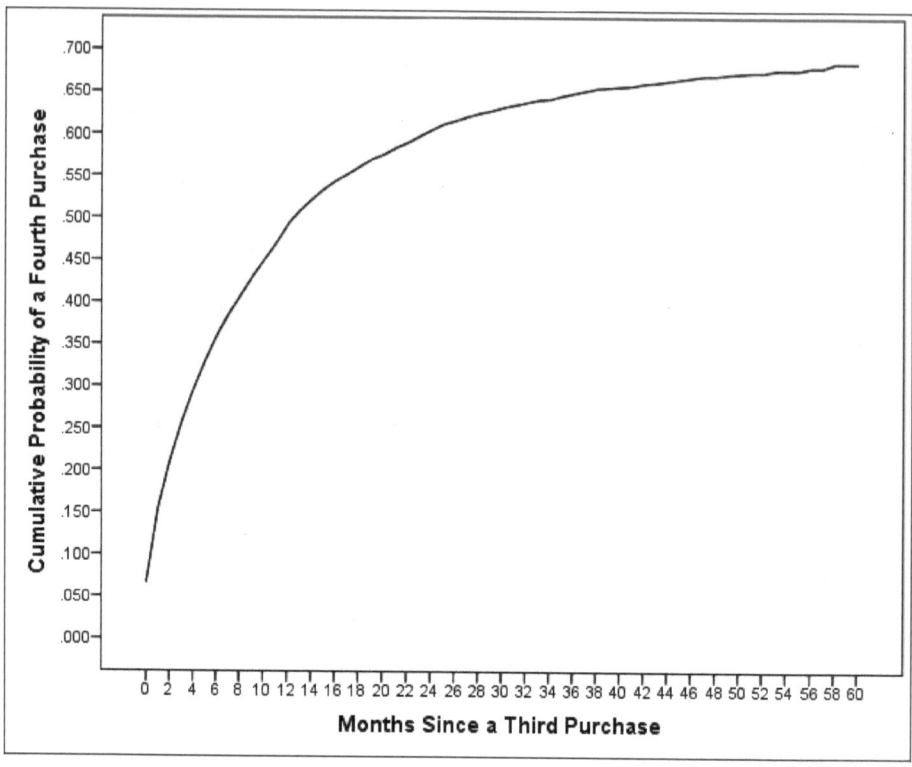

We are getting closer, aren't we?

The third-time buyer has a 49% chance of buying again in the next twelve-months, and a 69% chance of buying again in the next five years. Remember, my definition of a loyal customer is a customer who has a 60% chance of buying again in the next twelve months.

This is a long customer journey, isn't it? The customer has purchased for a third time. That's asking a lot out of the customer, don't you think? And yet, after three purchases, the probability of the customer buying again in the next year is no better or no worse than a coin flip.

Geez!

Here's the graph for customers who just placed a fourth purchase.

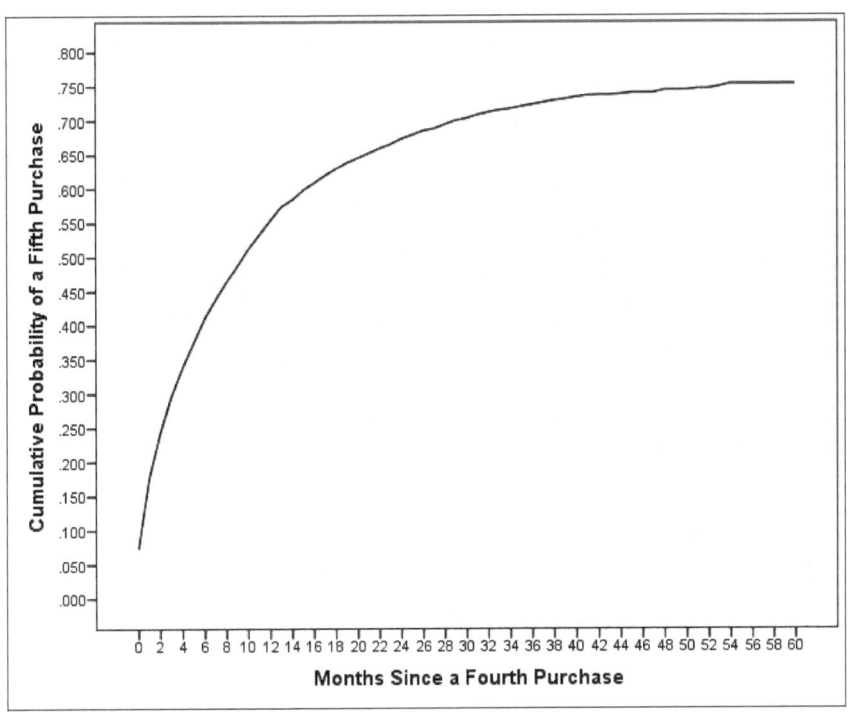

The customer who purchased for a fourth time has a 55% chance of buying again in the next twelve months, and a 75% chance of buying again in the next five years. We're getting very close to identifying a loyal customer, aren't we?

Here is the graph for a customer who just purchased for the fifth time.

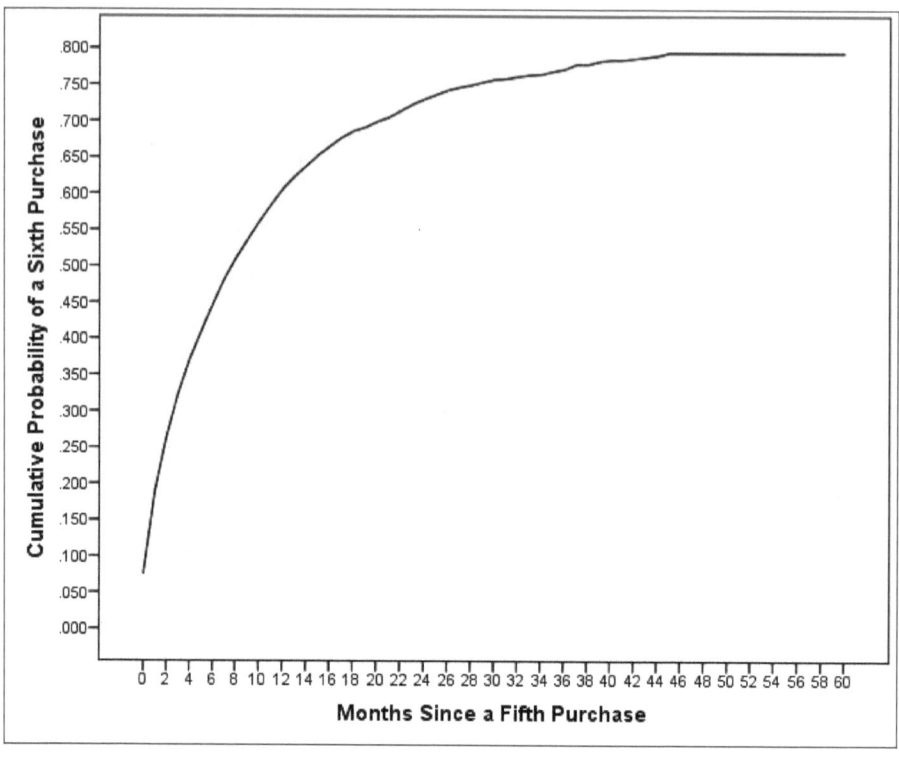

Look at this ... we've done it! The customer who just purchased for the fifth time has a 61% chance of buying again in the next year (and a 79% chance of buying again in the next five years).

In other words, it takes five life-to-date purchases for the customer to become "loyal" based on my definition.

This table illustrates the cumulative repurchase rates by month, for the first twenty-four months since a purchase.

	Monthly Cumulative Rebuy Rates				
Month	1x - 2x	2x - 3x	3x - 4x	4x - 5x	5x - 6x
0	4.1%	5.5%	6.6%	7.4%	7.5%
1	8.6%	13.0%	15.4%	17.8%	18.9%
2	11.2%	17.5%	21.0%	24.3%	26.3%
3	13.4%	21.1%	25.7%	29.6%	32.3%
4	15.1%	24.0%	29.5%	33.8%	37.1%
5	16.6%	26.5%	32.8%	37.4%	40.9%
6	18.0%	28.9%	35.8%	41.0%	44.6%
7	19.2%	31.0%	38.4%	43.8%	48.1%
8	20.3%	32.8%	40.7%	46.4%	51.0%
9	21.3%	34.5%	43.0%	48.7%	53.6%
10	22.2%	36.2%	45.0%	51.1%	56.1%
11	23.2%	37.9%	47.0%	53.2%	58.4%
12	24.6%	39.8%	49.3%	55.3%	60.6%
13	25.4%	41.0%	50.9%	57.3%	62.3%
14	26.1%	42.1%	52.2%	58.4%	63.8%
15	26.6%	43.1%	53.4%	59.8%	65.3%
16	27.1%	44.0%	54.4%	60.8%	66.5%
17	27.6%	44.7%	55.2%	61.9%	67.7%
18	28.1%	45.4%	56.1%	62.9%	68.6%
19	28.5%	46.0%	57.0%	63.8%	69.1%
20	28.9%	46.7%	57.6%	64.5%	69.9%
21	29.2%	47.2%	58.4%	65.2%	70.5%
22	29.6%	47.8%	59.0%	65.9%	71.4%
23	30.0%	48.4%	59.8%	66.5%	72.3%
24	30.6%	49.1%	60.5%	67.3%	73.0%

As the customer journey progresses, the customer evolves … from a 25% chance of repurchasing in the year after a first purchase to a 40% chance of repurchasing in the year after a second purchase to a 49% chance of repurchasing in the year after a third purchase to a 55% chance of repurchasing in the year after a fourth purchase to a 61% chance of repurchasing in the year after a fifth purchase.

When looking at sixty-month repurchase rates, we learn (in this example) that customer medians for a repurchase tend to happen in six month increments. On average, then, it takes about thirty months for a customer to become loyal. That isn't a terribly long period of time, so that is good news. But the probabilities are so low that only 1 in 282 customers get to loyal status within thirty months. Maybe 3 or 4 in 100 ever become loyal.

Again, this is a typical e-commerce business.

We learned that the odds of a first-time buyer purchasing for a second time are low.

We learned that the customer has to purchase five times before the customer becomes loyal.

We learned that the odds of a customer becoming loyal are very low.

What happens when a customer finally becomes loyal?

Loyalty is Fleeting

For this business, I segmented customers based on life-to-date purchases, and by months since a last purchase. Then, I measured the percentage of customers who purchased in the next twelve months. Here's what the table looks like.

Recency	1x Buyers	2x Buyers	3x Buyers	4x Buyers	5x Buyers	6x Buyers	7x Buyers	8x Buyers
1	31.3%	45.2%	53.7%	54.2%	61.2%	66.1%	70.2%	73.5%
2	27.6%	43.5%	48.9%	53.8%	57.6%	58.9%	60.2%	
3	18.3%	30.5%	41.5%	46.8%	55.6%	55.7%	54.1%	
4	17.8%	33.8%	45.0%	44.7%	51.2%	53.3%		
5	19.1%	34.9%	46.4%	47.3%	50.7%			
6	19.0%	35.8%	47.0%	47.0%	49.9%			
7	18.0%	32.5%	40.3%	46.8%	48.1%			
8	16.0%	26.5%	43.5%	46.7%	44.5%			
9	15.7%	28.7%	34.4%	45.0%	46.5%			
10	15.8%	26.4%	40.5%	43.2%	44.4%			
11	12.5%	23.3%	37.0%	38.0%	48.7%			
12	13.1%	26.7%	35.5%	36.4%	43.8%			

This table illustrates the probability of a customer purchasing in the next twelve months, based on current recency/frequency attributes.

Read down the "5x Buyers" column. Here, the customer has a 61.2% chance of buying again in the next twelve months. The customer is loyal, according to my definition. Whew, finally!

But then a month goes by, and the customer does not repurchase.

What is the probability of a customer buying for a sixth time, given that the customer now possesses two months of recency? Just read down one additional row. The probability is 57.6%.

In other words, we had to wait for the customer to purchase for the fifth time for the customer becomes loyal. And once the customer becomes loyal, it only takes one month to pass before the customer is once again not loyal.

Read down the "7x Buyers" column. These customers just purchased for the 7th time. If recency = one month, then the customer has a 70% chance of buying again in the next year. If the customer slips one month, and possesses two months of recency, then the customer has a 60% chance of buying again in the next year … the customer clings to loyal status. But if the customer does not purchase again, then the customer drops to three months of recency, and is no longer loyal.

Loyalty status is very, very fleeting, indeed!

This is a common story. Customers are always in a state of transition. For the most part, customer loyalty erodes slowly over time. When a customer purchases, customer loyalty is briefly high, then begins to slowly erode once again.

The secret, then, is to understand when the customer is likely to slip down into a lower "Loyalty Phase", and take corresponding action.

Loyalty Phases

I like to segment my customer into five "Loyalty Phases". The phases are based on the probability of the customer purchasing again in the next twelve months. Each Loyalty Phase is labeled by a grade, just as if the customer were in school:

Loyalty Phase "A" = 80% or greater chance of buying again in the next twelve months.

Loyalty Phase "B" = 60% to 79% chance of buying again in the next twelve months.

Loyalty Phase "C" = 40% to 59% chance of buying again in the next twelve months.

Loyalty Phase "D" = 20% to 39% chance of buying again in the next twelve months.

Loyalty Phase "F" = 0% to 19% chance of buying again in the next twelve months.

For most businesses, there is going to be a high skew the distribution of customers. There will be very few "A" customers, there will be a ton of "F" customers.

I typically build a logistic regression model to calculate the probability of a customer purchasing again in the next twelve months. I calculate square root of months since last purchase, I measure life-to-date purchase frequency or annual purchase frequency variables. I use channel-based variables (i.e. search or affiliates or print or email marketing) to separate customers. I use average order values, or price per item purchased, or average number of items purchased per order as variables in the model. If I am analyzing a retail business, I will use distance to a store as a variable (it is common for customers who live five miles from a store to be more loyal than customers who live fifty-five miles from a store, for instance).

For instance, I built a very simple logistic regression equation for the business we are looking at. Here's the equation in our example:

$$\text{Logit} = -0.22 - 0.375 * \text{SQRT(Months Since Last Purchase)} + 0.272 * (\text{Average Order Value} / 1000) + 0.175 * (\text{Phone Orders}) + 0.162 * (\text{Online Orders}) + 0.228 * (\text{Email Orders}) + 0.207 * (\text{Search Orders}).$$

Annual Rebuy Rate $= \text{EXP(Logit)} / (1 + \text{EXP(Logit)})$.

Once the equation is built, you score the customer file as it exists today. The key is to identify customers who are about to fall out of one of your Loyalty Phases.

Here's an example. Let's evaluate a customer who just purchased for the first time, and purchased online, spending $100.

Simple Loyalty Equation		
		Values
Step 1:	Enter Recency	1
Step 2:	Enter Average Order Value	$100.00
Step 3:	Enter Phone Orders	0
Step 4:	Enter Online Orders	1
Step 5:	Enter Email Orders	0
Step 6:	Enter Search Orders	0
	Logit Value	(0.406)
	Annual Repurchase Rate	40.0%

The customer has a 40% chance of purchasing in the next year. Not bad for a first-time buyer, according to this model for an e-commerce business.

Now the customer fades to a recency of two months.

Simple Loyalty Equation

		Values
Step 1:	Enter Recency	2
Step 2:	Enter Average Order Value	$100.00
Step 3:	Enter Phone Orders	0
Step 4:	Enter Online Orders	1
Step 5:	Enter Email Orders	0
Step 6:	Enter Search Orders	0
	Logit Value	(0.561)
	Annual Repurchase Rate	36.3%

The annual repurchase rate dropped under 40% - the customer is now graded as a "D" customer, from a Loyalty Phase standpoint. The customer is quickly becoming less responsive.

At 14 months of recency (14 months since the last purchase), the annual repurchase rate drops below 20%. The customer just fell from a "D" Loyalty Phase to an "F" Loyalty Phase.

Simple Loyalty Equation

		Values
Step 1:	Enter Recency	14
Step 2:	Enter Average Order Value	$100.00
Step 3:	Enter Phone Orders	0
Step 4:	Enter Online Orders	1
Step 5:	Enter Email Orders	0
Step 6:	Enter Search Orders	0
	Logit Value	(1.434)
	Annual Repurchase Rate	19.2%

Of course, if the purchase had happened via email instead of online, the annual repurchase rate would be marginally different.

Simple Loyalty Equation		Values
Step 1:	Enter Recency	14
Step 2:	Enter Average Order Value	$100.00
Step 3:	Enter Phone Orders	0
Step 4:	Enter Online Orders	0
Step 5:	Enter Email Orders	1
Step 6:	Enter Search Orders	0
	Logit Value	(1.368)
	Annual Repurchase Rate	20.3%

There are many businesses that have significantly different annual repurchase rates based on the channel that the customer purchased from. Ten years ago, it was common for the retail in-store buyer to have a higher repurchase rate, all things being equal, than an online buyer. Today, the trend is equalizing, though in-store purchases carry significant weight.

Let's look at a customer who purchased online eight times, and has a recency of one month.

Simple Loyalty Equation

		Values
Step 1:	Enter Recency	1
Step 2:	Enter Average Order Value	$100.00
Step 3:	Enter Phone Orders	0
Step 4:	Enter Online Orders	8
Step 5:	Enter Email Orders	0
Step 6:	Enter Search Orders	0
	Logit Value	0.728
	Annual Repurchase Rate	67.4%

For this e-commerce business, a customer with eight historical purchases, one happening just one month ago, is deemed a loyal customer, and is in Loyalty Phase = "B".

Let's see what happens when recency changes to two months ago.

Simple Loyalty Equation

		Values
Step 1:	Enter Recency	2
Step 2:	Enter Average Order Value	$100.00
Step 3:	Enter Phone Orders	0
Step 4:	Enter Online Orders	8
Step 5:	Enter Email Orders	0
Step 6:	Enter Search Orders	0
	Logit Value	0.573
	Annual Repurchase Rate	63.9%

The drop is significant, isn't it? Loyalty is already fading. How about at three months of recency?

Simple Loyalty Equation

		Values
Step 1:	Enter Recency	3
Step 2:	Enter Average Order Value	$100.00
Step 3:	Enter Phone Orders	0
Step 4:	Enter Online Orders	8
Step 5:	Enter Email Orders	0
Step 6:	Enter Search Orders	0
	Logit Value	0.454
	Annual Repurchase Rate	61.2%

The customer is about to fall out of this Loyalty Phase. The customer is in the "B" phase, and is ready to drop out of my criteria for loyal status (> 60% annual repurchase rate). At four months of recency?

Simple Loyalty Equation

		Values
Step 1:	Enter Recency	4
Step 2:	Enter Average Order Value	$100.00
Step 3:	Enter Phone Orders	0
Step 4:	Enter Online Orders	8
Step 5:	Enter Email Orders	0
Step 6:	Enter Search Orders	0
	Logit Value	0.353
	Annual Repurchase Rate	58.7%

The customer just dropped under sixty percent, and is now in Loyalty Phase "C".

Let's assume that the customer remains inactive for two additional years. Recency is now equal to twenty-eight months.

Simple Loyalty Equation

		Values
Step 1:	Enter Recency	28
Step 2:	Enter Average Order Value	$100.00
Step 3:	Enter Phone Orders	0
Step 4:	Enter Online Orders	8
Step 5:	Enter Email Orders	0
Step 6:	Enter Search Orders	0
	Logit Value	(0.881)
	Annual Repurchase Rate	29.3%

This is fascinating, isn't it? The customer has an annual repurchase rate (29%) that is directionally similar to a first-time buyer with five months of recency (see below):

Simple Loyalty Equation

		Values
Step 1:	Enter Recency	5
Step 2:	Enter Average Order Value	$100.00
Step 3:	Enter Phone Orders	0
Step 4:	Enter Online Orders	1
Step 5:	Enter Email Orders	0
Step 6:	Enter Search Orders	0
	Logit Value	(0.869)
	Annual Repurchase Rate	29.5%

A customer with eight life-to-date purchases but no purchases in twenty-eight months is equal to a first-time buyer who has not purchased in five months (in this example).

The key takeaway is that when a long-time, loyal buyer lapses, you don't give up on the customer. You keep plugging along, trying to encourage the customer to purchase. Think about this from an email marketing standpoint. There are factions out there that recommend not sending email campaigns to non-responsive customers. Think about the logic of that tactic. You have an outbound marketing tactic that could help convert a previously loyal customer back to loyal status, and instead, you will stop emailing the customer (who opted-in in the first place) because the customer is not "engaged"? Nonsense.

You know just how hard it is to move a customer along to loyal status. It is terribly hard work, and the odds are not in your favor.

Furthermore, if you are given a choice to upgrade/reactivate two seemingly equal customers, it is usually better to reactivate the customer who used to be highly loyal. Look below – the first example shows the predicted annual repurchase rate for a 2nd time buyer, and for a 9th time buyer.

Simple Loyalty Equation

		Values
Step 1:	Enter Recency	1
Step 2:	Enter Average Order Value	$100.00
Step 3:	Enter Phone Orders	0
Step 4:	Enter Online Orders	2
Step 5:	Enter Email Orders	0
Step 6:	Enter Search Orders	0
	Logit Value	(0.244)
	Annual Repurchase Rate	43.9%

Simple Loyalty Equation

		Values
Step 1:	Enter Recency	1
Step 2:	Enter Average Order Value	$100.00
Step 3:	Enter Phone Orders	0
Step 4:	Enter Online Orders	9
Step 5:	Enter Email Orders	0
Step 6:	Enter Search Orders	0
	Logit Value	0.890
	Annual Repurchase Rate	70.9%

In most cases, you obtain more benefit by reactivating the previously loyal buyer than you obtain by reactivating a less loyal buyer, even if current annual repurchase rate predictions are equal. But your mileage may vary. What matters is that you run the math, and that you understand how loyal customers reactivate.

Actionable Loyalty Phases

Look at the table below. These are customer counts by Loyalty Phase, by months since last purchase (for the e-commerce business we are analyzing):

Recency	Loyalty Phase = "A"	Loyalty Phase = "B"	Loyalty Phase = "C"	Loyalty Phase = "D"	Loyalty Phase = "F"
1	1,049	759	1,701	1,518	0
2	832	532	1,179	1,947	0
3	982	810	1,728	5,440	0
4	775	587	1,368	3,657	0
5	570	468	923	2,989	0
6	600	508	1,057	3,250	0
7	465	385	872	3,617	0
8	366	308	684	3,373	0
9	385	342	906	3,661	546
10	261	290	652	2,630	1,625
11	229	229	578	2,268	1,818
12	218	240	611	2,161	1,778
13 to 24	736	901	2,443	13,206	39,862
25 to 36	120	170	522	3,814	57,475
37 to 48	25	34	72	612	45,642
49 to 60	8	7	20	151	42,320
61+ Mo.	4	4	8	50	152,263
Totals	7,625	6,574	15,324	54,344	343,329

There are 7,625 customers in Loyalty Phase "A" – meaning that they have at least an 80% chance of purchasing again in the next year. These are the most loyal buyers. Couple them with the 6,574 customers in Loyalty Phase "B" (a 60% to 79% chance of buying again in the next year), and you have nearly 14,000 "loyal" buyers in the database.

If you were compelled to run a loyalty program of some sort, this is the audience that deserves to be part of the program. This audience has at least a 60% chance of buying again in the next year, so if you can increase their response by 10%, you'll have a meaningful chance of generating enough business to cover the costs of your loyalty program.

There are 15,324 customers in Loyalty Phase = "C" … with a 40% to 59% chance of purchasing again in the next twelve months. These customers are "on the fence" – they are clearly good customers, but they are not great customers. With one or two additional purchases, these customers may become loyal. While it may seem like it is easy to convert a customer to purchase one or two more times, it isn't. It is terribly hard work.

Loyalty Program Profitability

It is rare that I analyze a loyalty program that delivers sufficient profit to pay for the costs of the program. Not impossible, mind you, but rare.

Why?

It's simple math.

Let's say that you create a program for all customers in your database who have at least a 60% chance of repurchasing in the next year. You offer these customers a special 15% off promotion on all purchases, and you offer the customer free shipping on all purchases. Wow, good stuff! And customers respond accordingly.

But let's also assume that you executed a test – you split the loyalty audience in half, with half of the audience not allowed to participate in the loyalty program. The other audience does not earn 15% off each purchase, and the other audience only gets free shipping on all orders > $100.

At the end of the year, you run a profit and loss statement on each segment. Take a look at the profit and loss statement below. What do you observe?

Impact of a Loyalty Program

	Loyalty Program	Business As Is	Incremental Gain
Beginning Buyers	4,000	4,000	
Annual Rebuy Rate	75.0%	70.0%	
Orders per Repurchaser	3.50	3.00	
Average Order Value	$113.34	$113.10	
Gross Sales	$1,400,083	$1,050,044	$350,039
Less Discounts	($210,013)	($100,004)	($110,009)
Net Sales	$1,190,070	$950,040	$240,030
Cost of Goods Sold	($630,037)	($472,520)	($157,517)
Gross Margin	$560,033	$477,520	$82,513
Less Advertising Expense	($150,000)	($150,000)	$0
Less Shipping Expense	($119,007)	($95,004)	($24,003)
Add Shipping Revenue	$0	$114,005	($114,005)
Other Shipping Expenses	($59,504)	($47,502)	($12,002)
Variable Profit	$231,522	$299,019	($67,497)
Less Fixed Costs	($95,004)	($95,004)	$0
Earnings Before Taxes	$136,518	$204,015	($67,497)
EBT % of Net Sales	11.5%	21.5%	

My goodness, this is a catastrophe!

This, by the way, is the way many of the profit and loss statements look when I analyze loyalty programs.

By giving everybody 15% off, and by giving everybody free shipping on all orders, we get a lot of benefits. Repurchase rates increase from 70% to 75%. We increase orders per repurchaser from 3.0 to 3.5. The loyalty program made a difference!

The loyalty program increased total demand by 25%. We generated $1,190,070 instead of $950,040. Wow!

That's the good news.

Here's the problem.

We gave away too much to generate the sales increase. Gross margins declined, simply because we had to discount merchandise in order to get loyal buyers to spend more. Shipping expenses increased, because we shipped more merchandise to the customer. Shipping revenue decreased, because we gave loyal buyers free shipping (i.e. no revenue). We needed to hire more people to pick/pack/ship orders among the loyalty program segment, because there were more orders to ship, yielding more expense.

When we run the math, we are confronted with an uncomfortable truth. The loyalty program cost the company money. We were able to increase customer loyalty, but we decreased company profit in the process.

Why would we ever want to decrease company profitability? The goal of business is to increase company profitability. Without profit (cash), we are out of business.

We can run different scenarios. Is there a scenario that increases profitability? The answer is "yes".

Impact of a Loyalty Program			
	Loyalty Program	Business As Is	Incremental Gain
Beginning Buyers	4,000	4,000	
Annual Rebuy Rate	75.0%	70.0%	
Orders per Repurchaser	4.15	3.00	
Average Order Value	$113.34	$113.10	
Gross Sales	$1,660,098	$1,050,044	$610,054
Less Discounts	($249,015)	($100,004)	($149,011)
Net Sales	$1,411,083	$950,040	$461,043
Cost of Goods Sold	($747,044)	($472,520)	($274,524)
Gross Margin	$664,039	$477,520	$186,519
Less Advertising Expense	($150,000)	($150,000)	$0
Less Shipping Expense	($141,108)	($95,004)	($46,104)
Add Shipping Revenue	$0	$114,005	($114,005)
Other Shipping Expenses	($70,554)	($47,502)	($23,052)
Variable Profit	$302,376	$299,019	$3,357
Less Fixed Costs	($95,004)	($95,004)	$0
Earnings Before Taxes	$207,372	$204,015	$3,357
EBT % of Net Sales	14.7%	21.5%	

Look at the difference in net sales. That's a huge difference, isn't it?

In this case, we must achieve a 49% increase in net sales in order for profit to increase.

This is the problem with loyalty programs.

It is possible to increase sales.

But the expense required to increase sales is significant – often too significant to cover the cost of the program. As a result, loyalty programs frequently lose money.

In my example, it took a 49% increase in net sales to drive a profit increase.

In my consulting work, it is common to see a 15% increase in net sales from loyalty initiatives. The problem, then, is that it costs too much in terms of rewards to generate the 15% increase in net sales.

Worse, many of my clients know this. As a result, they reverse engineer the profit and loss statement, seeking to find the magical point where the profit and loss statement works. My clients do extensive work, only to learn that the profit and loss statement works when a 15% increase in net sales is paired with a 3% - 5% increase in expense.

One problem.

A 3% - 5% increase in expense seldom yields a 15% increase in net sales.

It is common to match a dollar of expense with three or four dollars of net sales. When this happens, the transaction can be profitable. Unfortunately, points and percentage off deals and free shipping struggle to generate this level of return.

The One Metric That Dictates Your Marketing Strategy

I have analyzed more than 200 brands since founding MineThatData back in 2007. During that time, the average annual repurchase rate among customers who purchased in the past year is about 35%.

Let that number sink in for a moment. Across a diverse client base of billion dollar brands, plucky startups, and global businesses, only 35% of last year's buyer file will purchase again this year.

Yes, that's the average.

How are those businesses going to grow? Let's say they find a way to make the existing customer base far more loyal, and instead of 35% of last year's buyer file purchasing again this year, 45% of last year's buyer file purchases again this year. The business, still, with spectacular growth in customer loyalty, must replace more than half of last year's buyer file with new + reactivated buyers (mostly new).

About 80% of my client base possesses an annual repurchase rate under 40%. And if the customer purchases again, the customer purchases somewhere between 1.5 and 2.0 times in the next year.

When I worked at Nordstrom, a decade ago now, we retained 75% of last year's buyer file. If a customer purchased again, the customer purchased six times in the next year.

Think about the difference between the average business I analyze, and Nordstrom.

The average business can expect to generate 0.35 * 1.75 = 0.61 purchases this year from last year's buyer.

Nordstrom, back in the day, could expect to generate 0.75*6.00 = 4.50 purchases this year from last year's buyer.

It should not be surprising that Nordstrom cultivated a loyal buyer file over the years. The loyal buyer file feeds upon itself, generating a ton of profit for the brand, generating word-of-mouth that brings new customers into the fold.

It should not be surprising that the average business possesses loyal buyers, but does not possess a loyal buyer file. The average business must constantly find a steady flow of low cost new customers, in order to simply maintain sales levels from year to year.

The key, then, is to simply measure your annual repurchase rate. Identify every customer who purchased in 2014, and simply measure the percentage of customers who purchase again during 2015.

If you find that 60% or more of 2014 buyers purchase again during 2015, you have a fighting chance to make loyalty programs work.

If you find that, like the majority of my client base, 35% of 2014 buyers purchase again during 2015, then your entire focus needs to be on finding low-cost new buyers … lots of 'em!!!

This one metric determines your marketing strategy.

But here's what usually happens. We are told stories about things that Starbucks or Nordstrom or Delta or Target do to "engage" their most loyal buyers. Well, why do you think we are told these stories? It's simple, really. Those companies retain more than 60% of last year's buyer file.

You do not hear stories about how the garden variety brand with a 35% annual repurchase rate generates customer loyalty – and for good reason – those companies are not going to be able to generate scalable customer loyalty.

It is also interesting that the most successful loyalty programs find ways to offer customer benefits without having to spend money on the benefits. When I worked at Nordstrom, we used our Anniversary Sale as a tactic to drive loyal customer behavior. For two weeks in late July, we offered Fall merchandise at about 20% off (to everybody) – and the tactic yielded sales levels comparable to Christmas. It was complete madness, folks!! About a month prior to the sale, we sent notification to our better customers, those who spent $750 in the past year and were proprietary credit customers. These customers were offered a perk. They could come in to our stores a full week prior to the sale, and pick and choose any merchandise they desired. The merchandise would be held for them. On the first day of the sale, our loyal customers would waltz past the crazed masses. Our loyal customers would meet with their personal sales associate, they'd pick up the merchandise they reserved a week prior, pay for it, and leave the store.

It was common to see a gain of $100 per loyal customer, compared to a control group. That is a stunningly high number, friends.

How much did the program cost? Almost nothing. We simply had to spend money to notify our best customers. We'd spend $0.45 on a post card and $0 on email, generating $100 of sales and $28 profit in the process. $28 of profit scales well against $0.45 marketing cost.

Mind you, all customers were paying the same price for the merchandise. It wasn't like we were offering best customers lower prices. If I remember correctly, we may have offered double or triple points within the credit program, so there was a cost associated with that (a few dollars, tops).

So even with a highly loyal customer base, and a 75% annual repurchase rate, the secret to loyalty success was to find emotional benefits that yielded sales increases at low cost.

When you fly United, you can see the impact of low cost emotional benefits. Fly often? You are getting on the airplane first, and your luggage is with you. Fly infrequently? God help you, because you are boarding twenty minutes later, and your luggage won't be with you. Fly often? You can convert your points into upgrades in Economy Plus – you get more room at no cost to United. You can ask for a free upgrade to First Class, and your free upgrade is prioritized based on loyalty status. Again, you earn emotional benefits at no cost to United. You have to fly with United almost monthly just to earn the right to earn these benefits. And each time you exchange miles for emotional perks, you do not use miles for free flights.

I have learned that there are two secrets to business success.

First, if your business retains 60% or more of last year's twelve-month buyer file, be certain to offer emotional rewards that generate minimal marketing expense.

Second, if you are like most companies, you possess customers who have less than a 40% chance of purchasing again in the next twelve months. Your success has nothing to do with increasing customer loyalty. Your success has everything to do with finding new/infrequent buyers at a low cost.

Make sense?

I'm not saying that loyalty programs don't work.

I am saying that the vast majority of businesses do not possess a loyal customer file, and that is not the fault of the business. Be honest, how many times a year do you need to shop at Ann Taylor? Two? There's no amount of marketing wizardry that will cause you to need to shop at Ann Taylor every-other-week. Most of the businesses we work for do not offer products and services that are needed all the time. If you work for Wal-Mart or Amazon or Starbucks, then of course, your customers are buying all the time. You can do things to impact customer loyalty. But if you work for Blinds.com, well, just how often does the customer need blinds?

More of e-commerce / retail falls into the Blinds.com category than into the Amazon category.

Think about social media for a moment. You're constantly told that you have to get customers to engage with your brand. Well, if you are Facebook or Google, absolutely! Your customer is spending a half-hour a day with you, so engagement is important. If you are Blinds.com, just how the heck do you think you're going to get customers to engage with you? And even if you somehow achieve the nearly impossible task of boosting engagement, what do you get for it? The customer only needs blinds every "x" years, right?

Everything comes down to two rules.

First, if your business retains 60% or more of last year's twelve-month buyer file, be certain to offer emotional rewards that generate minimal marketing expense.

Second, if you are like most companies, you possess customers who have less than a 40% chance of purchasing again in the next twelve months. Your success has nothing to do with increasing customer loyalty. Your success has everything to do with finding new/infrequent buyers at a low cost.

Which business do you work for?

Overspending

When you start a business, odds are you aren't flush in cash. Sure, maybe you have venture funding, but that money is used to find new customers. Not much is spent marketing to existing customers. Maybe a few emails or texts, or a customer service phone call. In the early days, it has to be this way.

Interestingly, in the early stages of a business, there are customers who exhibit loyal behavior. These customers purchase multiple times per year, and they evangelize the brand to others.

When a business matures, the relationship between best customers and marketing changes. It becomes harder to acquire new customers – you reach a level where customers and marketing spend and profitability optimize. At that point, growth becomes very hard. Very, very hard! When growth stalls, marketers look to the existing customer base.

All existing and inexpensive channels are maximized first. Email frequency goes up from two per week to five per week.

Then discounts and promotions are offered. Free shipping with a hurdle. Then free shipping with no hurdle. Then ten percent off plus free shipping, followed by twenty percent off, and twenty-five percent off. Then it is fifty percent off on specific items and twenty percent off everything else. Eventually, print is used to notify customers of the discounts and promotions, tacking on thirty-five cents of notification expense.

It is not uncommon for a mature business with a strong desire to market to existing customers to spend $40 of marketing and discounting and free shipping expense per $100 of sales. Let that one sink in for a moment. Especially if you are dealing with a catalog brand – those folks will mail a catalog every other week in an effort to drive volume. The e-commerce folks spend money via Google and Facebook and Affiliates. The dollars really pile up!

Remember when I talked about when a business is launched? Not much is spent marketing to existing customers. The demand generated by existing customers is what I call "organic demand". Demand is generated because the customer loves the combination of merchandise and value proposition. It is the most profitable demand a business can generate.

Across most of the businesses I analyze, roughly half of demand from existing buyers is "organic", with the remainder generated by marketing activities. When I worked at Nordstrom, more than 90% of demand was organic. You'll find that the best companies are able to get customers to buy merchandise without the need for marketing activities. You'll find that the absolute smartest marketers are needed to generate optimal levels of profit via marketing activities. You'll find that most companies overspend on marketing activities. When you overspend on existing customers, you have less money to spend on new customers. When you don't have enough money to spend on new customers, you don't have the ability to grow as fast as you otherwise could. Maybe worst of all, when somebody recommends spending less on existing customers, there will be a group of Executives who strongly believe that if you spend less on existing customers, then existing customers will spend less, and the business will suffer. This form of logic, right or wrong, leads to bloated levels of marketing spend among existing customers.

Should We Spend Marketing Dollars On Existing Buyers?

Let's look at an example. I created a simulation tool that allows me to estimate the long-term impact of spending too much or too little on existing buyers and new buyers.

The spreadsheet simulation can be found here: http://minethatdata.com/Kevin_Hillstrom_MineThatData_Loyalty_LTV.xlsx

I'll show you what the first five years of the simulation look like (if it is difficult to read the text in print, please refer to the spreadsheet on your laptop / tablet, where you'll be able to easily read the figures in the table):

Lifetime Value and Customer Loyalty Worksheet

Author = Kevin Hillstrom, President, MineThatData

Recency	Grade	Mkt. $	Mkt. Chg.	Organic %	Today	After Year 1	After Year 2	After Year 3	After Year 4	After Year 5
0 to 12	A	$40.00	1.000	75.0%	83,747	88,199	92,079	95,395	98,230	100,688
	B	$32.00	1.000	67.0%	83,788	88,094	91,383	94,110	96,450	98,532
	C	$25.00	1.000	60.0%	82,517	85,569	87,941	89,950	91,691	93,284
	D	$20.00	1.000	55.0%	83,857	85,469	86,881	88,168	89,342	90,431
	F	$15.00	1.000	50.0%	73,270	74,152	75,030	75,872	76,666	77,425
13 to 24		$10.00	1.000	46.0%	269,583	273,959	282,426	289,429	295,501	300,840
25 to 36		$6.00	1.000	42.0%	206,324	234,120	237,920	245,273	251,355	256,628
37 to 48		$4.00	1.000	38.0%	165,596	191,887	217,738	221,272	228,111	233,767
49 to 60		$3.00	1.000	34.0%	147,040	158,460	183,618	208,354	211,737	218,281
61+		$2.00	1.000	30.0%	600,763	734,635	877,587	1,042,836	1,229,637	1,416,902
Newbies	Free	$0.00	1.000	100.0%	43,611	43,611	43,611	43,611	43,611	43,611
	Paid	$20.00	1.000	0.0%	174,445	174,445	174,445	174,445	174,445	174,445

						After Year 1	After Year 2	After Year 3	After Year 4	After Year 5
		Merchandise Productivity				1.000	1.000	1.000	1.000	1.000
		Profit Factor		40.0%		40.0%	40.0%	40.0%	40.0%	40.0%
		New Names Free =		20.0%						
		House Power =		0.500		After	After	After	After	After
		Acquisition Power =		0.700		Year 1	Year 2	Year 3	Year 4	Year 5
		Annual Demand			$88,376	$92,283	$95,670	$98,564	$101,060	$103,260
		Annual Buyers			407,179	421,482	433,313	443,495	452,379	460,360
		Marketing Cost			$20,271	$21,470	$22,525	$23,459	$24,300	$25,076
		Variable Op. Profit			$15,079	$15,447	$15,742	$15,967	$16,124	$16,228
		Profit % of Demand			17.1%	16.7%	16.5%	16.2%	16.0%	15.7%
		Demand per Buyer			$217.04	$218.97	$220.79	$222.24	$223.40	$224.30
		Cumm Demand				$92,293	$187,963	$286,527	$387,587	$490,846
		Cumm Profit				$15,447	$31,190	$47,156	$63,280	$79,508

The spreadsheet calculates out for ten years – but I want the printed numbers to be as large as possible so that you can read them.

The purple numbers are the numbers that I change.

This is a business that spends overwhelming amounts of money on existing buyers, spending way, way, waaaaaaaayyyyyyy too much money marketing to existing buyers!

Recall earlier I graded Loyalty Phases with A/B/C/D/F levels, based on annual repurchase rates. In this simulation tool, I use a different methodology to grade customers via A/B/C/D/F levels. Essentially, I divide twelve month buyers into equal groups of 20%, based on future spending potential.

Behind the scenes (cells A100 – I111), I input all of the data that defines how customers behave, on an annual basis.

In cells E6 – E17, I allow the user to change the organic percentage for each customer segment. Remember, the organic percentage is the fraction of annual demand that the customer will generate without the aid of any marketing activities whatsoever. The organic percentage drives the simulation, so do not get the organic percentage wrong, ok?!!

In cells D6 – D17, you can change the fraction of investment in each segment. If you want to decrease spend by 15%, enter a value of 0.85 in the cell you wish to adjust.

In cells F25 – P25, you see how much demand you generate, annually (in thousands).

In cells F26 – P26, you see how many customers purchase, annually.

In cells F27 – P27, you see how much you spent on marketing, annually.

In cells F28 – P28, you see how much profit you generated, prior to fixed costs (called "variable profit").

As you can see, this is a business that is forecast to grow modestly (top-line demand). Marketing costs are forecast to grow somewhat as well. Variable profit, however, is largely tepid. This business is essentially stuck.

Alright, let's document our base case. For the next five years, here is what profit looks like:

	Base Case	
	Demand	Profit
Today	$88,376	$15,079
Year 1	$92,293	$15,447
Year 2	$95,670	$15,742
Year 3	$98,564	$15,967
Year 4	$101,060	$16,124
Year 5	$103,260	$16,228
Tot: Yr 1-5	$490,847	$79,508

Ok, let's run a scenario, and see how the business changes. Let's change cell D6 from 1.00 to 1.10. We will increase spend among the best twelve-month buyers (graded as "A") by 10%. What happens over time?

Lifetime Value and Customer Loyalty Worksheet

Author = Kevin Hillstrom, President, MineThatData

Recency	Grade	Mkt. $	Mkt. Chg.	Organic %	Today	After Year 1	After Year 2	After Year 3	After Year 4	After Year 5
0 to 12	A	$40.00	1.100	75.0%	83,747	88,734	92,922	96,434	99,403	101,959
	B	$32.00	1.000	67.0%	83,788	88,207	91,559	94,336	96,716	98,829
	C	$25.00	1.000	60.0%	82,517	85,570	87,930	89,938	91,682	93,281
	D	$20.00	1.000	55.0%	83,857	85,469	86,870	88,154	89,327	90,416
	F	$15.00	1.000	50.0%	73,270	74,152	75,025	75,865	76,657	77,416
13 to 24		$10.00	1.000	46.0%	269,583	273,308	281,998	289,094	295,233	300,621
25 to 36		$6.00	1.000	42.0%	206,324	234,120	237,355	244,902	251,064	256,395
37 to 48		$4.00	1.000	38.0%	165,596	191,887	217,738	220,747	227,765	233,497
49 to 60		$3.00	1.000	34.0%	147,040	158,460	183,618	208,354	211,234	217,950
61+		$2.00	1.000	30.0%	600,763	734,635	877,587	1,042,836	1,229,637	1,416,413
Newbies	Free	$0.00	1.000	100.0%	43,611	43,611	43,611	43,611	43,611	43,611
	Paid	$20.00	1.000	0.0%	174,445	174,445	174,445	174,445	174,445	174,445

						After Year 1	After Year 2	After Year 3	After Year 4	After Year 5
			Merchandise Productivity			1.000	1.000	1.000	1.000	1.000
			Profit Factor		40.0%	40.0%	40.0%	40.0%	40.0%	40.0%
			New Names Free =		20.0%					
			House Power =		0.500	After Year 1	After Year 2	After Year 3	After Year 4	After Year 5
			Acquisition Power =		0.700					
			Annual Demand		$88,376	$92,649	$96,226	$99,250	$101,836	$104,102
			Annual Buyers		407,179	422,133	434,306	444,727	453,786	461,901
			Marketing Cost		$20,271	$21,805	$22,899	$23,862	$24,727	$25,521
			Variable Op. Profit		$15,079	$15,254	$15,592	$15,838	$16,008	$16,120
			Profit % of Demand		17.1%	16.5%	16.2%	16.0%	15.7%	15.5%
			Demand per Buyer		$217.04	$219.48	$221.56	$223.17	$224.42	$225.38
			Cumm Demand			$92,649	$188,875	$288,125	$389,961	$494,063
			Cumm Profit			$15,254	$30,846	$46,684	$62,692	$78,812

It looks like profit actually decreases, while top-line demand increases.

	Base Case		Adjusted Case	
	Demand	Profit	Demand	Profit
Today	$88,376	$15,079	$88,376	$15,079
Year 1	$92,293	$15,447	$92,649	$15,254
Year 2	$95,670	$15,742	$96,226	$15,592
Year 3	$98,564	$15,967	$99,250	$15,838
Year 4	$101,060	$16,124	$101,836	$16,008
Year 5	$103,260	$16,228	$104,102	$16,120
Tot: Yr 1-5	$490,847	$79,508	$494,063	$78,812
Change			$3,216	($696)
Growth			0.7%	-0.9%

44

This is a classic story. You can spend money marketing to loyal buyers, and top-line demand increases, but profit decreases. Clearly, it is not a good idea (if the goal of this business is to optimize profit) to spend more trying to get the very best customers to become even more loyal. Additional marketing spend is obviously sub-optimal for this segment.

As an FYI, I use a power function in the spreadsheet to estimate diminishing returns from marketing expenditures. The relationship is more linear in customer acquisition, it is more curved in housefile. If you would like more detail on the laws of diminishing returns, please send me an email message (kevinh@minethatdata.com), and I will give you additional details.

Ok, let's start working in the other direction. Here is what happens if marketing spend is cut by 10%.

Lifetime Value and Customer Loyalty Worksheet

Author = Kevin Hillstrom, President, MineThatData

Recency	Grade	Mkt. $	Mkt. Chg.	Organic %	Today	After Year 1	After Year 2	After Year 3	After Year 4	After Year 5
0 to 12	A	$40.00	0.900	75.0%	83,747	87,636	91,200	94,317	97,018	99,380
	B	$32.00	1.000	67.0%	83,788	87,974	91,199	93,875	96,176	98,226
	C	$25.00	1.000	60.0%	82,517	85,567	87,953	89,963	91,699	93,286
	D	$20.00	1.000	55.0%	83,857	85,469	86,892	88,183	89,358	90,446
	F	$15.00	1.000	50.0%	73,270	74,152	75,036	75,880	76,675	77,434
13 to 24		$10.00	1.000	46.0%	269,583	274,643	282,867	289,771	306,772	301,000
25 to 36		$6.00	1.000	42.0%	206,324	234,120	238,514	245,656	251,652	256,864
37 to 48		$4.00	1.000	38.0%	165,596	191,887	217,738	221,825	228,467	234,043
49 to 60		$3.00	1.000	34.0%	147,040	158,460	183,618	208,354	212,265	218,621
61+		$2.00	1.000	30.0%	600,763	734,635	877,587	1,042,836	1,229,637	1,417,416
Newbies	Free	$0.00	1.000	100.0%	43,611	43,611	43,611	43,611	43,611	43,611
	Paid	$20.00	1.000	0.0%	174,445	174,445	174,445	174,445	174,445	174,445

Merchandise Productivity		1.000	1.000	1.000	1.000	1.000
Profit Factor	40.0%	40.0%	40.0%	40.0%	40.0%	40.0%
New Names Free =	20.0%					
House Power =	0.500	After	After	After	After	After
Acquisition Power =	0.700	Year 1	Year 2	Year 3	Year 4	Year 5

	Today	After Year 1	After Year 2	After Year 3	After Year 4	After Year 5
Annual Demand	$88,376	$91,920	$95,089	$97,852	$100,259	$102,393
Annual Buyers	407,179	420,798	432,278	442,218	450,926	458,773
Marketing Cost	$20,271	$21,135	$22,155	$23,062	$23,881	$24,639
Variable Op. Profit	$15,079	$15,633	$15,880	$16,079	$16,222	$16,318
Profit % of Demand	17.1%	17.0%	16.7%	16.4%	16.2%	15.9%
Demand per Buyer	$217.04	$218.44	$219.97	$221.28	$222.34	$223.19
Cumm Demand		$91,920	$187,009	$284,861	$385,120	$487,513
Cumm Profit		$15,633	$31,513	$47,592	$63,815	$80,133

	Base Case		Adjusted Case	
	Demand	Profit	Demand	Profit
Today	$88,376	$15,079	$88,376	$15,079
Year 1	$92,293	$15,447	$91,920	$15,633
Year 2	$95,670	$15,742	$95,089	$15,880
Year 3	$98,564	$15,967	$97,852	$16,079
Year 4	$101,060	$16,124	$100,259	$16,222
Year 5	$103,260	$16,228	$102,393	$16,318
Tot: Yr 1-5	$490,847	$79,508	$487,513	$80,133
Change			($3,334)	$625
Growth			-0.7%	0.8%

The business is more profitable, but demand does decrease over time.

If the goal is to be more profitable, we can keep cutting. Let's reduce spend by 20%.

Lifetime Value and Customer Loyalty Worksheet

Author = Kevin Hillstrom, President, MineThatData

Recency	Grade	Mkt. $	Mkt. Chg.	Organic %	Today	After Year 1	After Year 2	After Year 3	After Year 4	After Year 5
0 to 12	A	$40.00	0.800	75.0%	83,747	87,042	90,278	93,195	95,761	98,027
	B	$32.00	1.000	67.0%	83,788	87,848	91,006	93,631	95,891	97,909
	C	$25.00	1.000	60.0%	82,517	85,564	87,965	89,976	91,708	93,289
	D	$20.00	1.000	55.0%	83,857	85,469	86,903	88,199	89,375	90,462
	F	$15.00	1.000	50.0%	73,270	74,152	75,042	75,888	76,684	77,443
13 to 24		$10.00	1.000	46.0%	269,583	275,367	283,323	290,120	296,048	301,284
25 to 36		$6.00	1.000	42.0%	206,324	234,120	239,143	246,052	251,955	257,104
37 to 48		$4.00	1.000	38.0%	165,596	191,887	217,738	222,409	228,835	234,325
49 to 60		$3.00	1.000	34.0%	147,040	158,460	183,618	208,354	212,824	218,974
61+		$2.00	1.000	30.0%	600,763	734,635	877,587	1,042,836	1,229,637	1,417,960
Newbies	Free	$0.00	1.000	100.0%	43,611	43,611	43,611	43,611	43,611	43,611
	Paid	$20.00	1.000	0.0%	174,445	174,445	174,445	174,445	174,445	174,445

		Merchandise Productivity				1.000	1.000	1.000	1.000	1.000
		Profit Factor			40.0%	40.0%	40.0%	40.0%	40.0%	40.0%
		New Names Free =			20.0%					
		House Power =			0.500	After Year 1	After Year 2	After Year 3	After Year 4	After Year 5
		Acquisition Power =			0.700					
		Annual Demand			$88,376	$91,524	$94,481	$97,111	$99,428	$101,496
		Annual Buyers			407,179	420,075	431,194	440,888	449,418	457,131
		Marketing Cost			$20,271	$20,800	$21,789	$22,670	$23,469	$24,210
		Variable Op. Profit			$15,079	$15,810	$16,004	$16,174	$16,302	$16,389
		Profit % of Demand			17.1%	17.3%	16.9%	16.7%	16.4%	16.1%
		Demand per Buyer			$217.04	$217.88	$219.12	$220.26	$221.24	$222.03
		Cumm Demand				$91,524	$186,005	$283,117	$382,545	$484,041
		Cumm Profit				$15,810	$31,813	$47,988	$64,290	$80,678

Profit increases once again.

Let's see just how much we can reduce marketing spend by, in an effort to optimize profit. I will list each scenario, where I drop marketing spend by another ten percent.

70% spend level.

Lifetime Value and Customer Loyalty Worksheet

Author = Kevin Hillstrom, President, MineThatData

Recency	Grade	Mkt. $	Mkt. Chg.	Organic %	Today	After Year 1	After Year 2	After Year 3	After Year 4	After Year 5
0 to 12	A	$40.00	0.700	75.0%	83,747	86,408	89,307	92,019	94,450	96,620
	B	$32.00	1.000	67.0%	83,788	87,713	90,803	93,374	95,593	97,580
	C	$25.00	1.000	60.0%	82,517	85,562	87,978	89,989	91,717	93,291
	D	$20.00	1.000	55.0%	83,857	85,469	86,915	88,215	89,392	90,479
	F	$15.00	1.000	50.0%	73,270	74,152	75,048	75,897	76,693	77,453
13 to 24		$10.00	1.000	46.0%	269,583	276,137	283,797	290,480	296,330	301,511
25 to 36		$6.00	1.000	42.0%	206,324	234,120	239,811	246,464	252,268	257,348
37 to 48		$4.00	1.000	38.0%	165,596	191,887	217,738	223,031	229,218	234,616
49 to 60		$3.00	1.000	34.0%	147,040	158,460	183,618	208,354	213,420	219,340
61+		$2.00	1.000	30.0%	600,763	734,635	877,587	1,042,836	1,229,637	1,418,539
Newbies	Free	$0.00	1.000	100.0%	43,611	43,611	43,611	43,611	43,611	43,611
	Paid	$20.00	1.000	0.0%	174,445	174,445	174,445	174,445	174,445	174,445

			Merchandise Productivity			1.000	1.000	1.000	1.000	1.000
			Profit Factor		40.0%	40.0%	40.0%	40.0%	40.0%	40.0%
			New Names Free =		20.0%					
			House Power =		0.500	After	After	After	After	After
			Acquisition Power =		0.700	Year 1	Year 2	Year 3	Year 4	Year 5
			Annual Demand		$88,376	$91,104	$93,840	$96,335	$98,561	$100,564
			Annual Buyers		407,179	419,305	430,051	439,494	447,846	455,423
			Marketing Cost		$20,271	$20,465	$21,426	$22,285	$23,065	$23,789
			Variable Op. Profit		$15,079	$15,976	$16,110	$16,249	$16,360	$16,436
			Profit % of Demand		17.1%	17.5%	17.2%	16.9%	16.6%	16.3%
			Demand per Buyer		$217.04	$217.27	$218.21	$219.20	$220.08	$220.81
			Cumm Demand			$91,104	$184,943	$281,278	$379,839	$480,403
			Cumm Profit			$15,976	$32,086	$48,335	$64,695	$81,131

60% spend level.

Lifetime Value and Customer Loyalty Worksheet

Author = Kevin Hillstrom, President, MineThatData

Recency	Grade	Mkt. $	Mkt. Chg.	Organic %	Today	After Year 1	After Year 2	After Year 3	After Year 4	After Year 5
0 to 12	A	$40.00	0.600	75.0%	83,747	85,728	88,274	90,777	93,072	95,145
	B	$32.00	1.000	67.0%	83,788	87,568	90,586	93,103	95,280	97,234
	C	$25.00	1.000	60.0%	82,517	85,560	87,992	90,004	91,727	93,293
	D	$20.00	1.000	55.0%	83,857	85,469	86,928	88,233	89,410	90,497
	F	$15.00	1.000	50.0%	73,270	74,152	75,055	75,906	76,703	77,463
13 to 24		$10.00	1.000	46.0%	269,583	276,964	284,294	290,852	296,620	301,744
25 to 36		$6.00	1.000	42.0%	206,324	234,120	240,530	246,895	252,591	257,600
37 to 48		$4.00	1.000	38.0%	165,596	191,887	217,738	223,699	229,619	234,916
49 to 60		$3.00	1.000	34.0%	147,040	158,460	183,618	208,354	214,059	219,724
61+		$2.00	1.000	30.0%	600,763	734,635	877,587	1,042,836	1,229,637	1,419,160
Newbies	Free	$0.00	1.000	100.0%	43,611	43,611	43,611	43,611	43,611	43,611
	Paid	$20.00	1.000	0.0%	174,445	174,445	174,445	174,445	174,445	174,445

			Merchandise Productivity			1.000	1.000	1.000	1.000	1.000
			Profit Factor		40.0%	40.0%	40.0%	40.0%	40.0%	40.0%
			New Names Free =		20.0%					
			House Power =		0.500	After Year 1	After Year 2	After Year 3	After Year 4	After Year 5
			Acquisition Power =		0.700					
			Annual Demand		$88,376	$90,651	$93,158	$95,515	$97,649	$99,587
			Annual Buyers		407,179	418,477	428,835	438,023	446,192	453,632
			Marketing Cost		$20,271	$20,130	$21,068	$21,906	$22,668	$23,377
			Variable Op. Profit		$15,079	$16,130	$16,195	$16,300	$16,392	$16,457
			Profit % of Demand		17.1%	17.8%	17.4%	17.1%	16.8%	16.5%
			Demand per Buyer		$217.04	$216.62	$217.23	$218.06	$218.85	$219.53
			Cumm Demand			$90,651	$183,809	$279,325	$376,974	$476,561
			Cumm Profit			$16,130	$32,326	$48,626	$65,018	$81,475

The 50% spend level is next.

Lifetime Value and Customer Loyalty Worksheet

Author = Kevin Hillstrom, President, MineThatData

Recency	Grade	Mkt. $	Mkt. Chg.	Organic %	Today	After Year 1	After Year 2	After Year 3	After Year 4	After Year 5
0 to 12	A	$40.00	0.500	75.0%	83,747	84,988	87,163	89,451	91,608	93,585
	B	$32.00	1.000	67.0%	83,788	87,411	90,354	92,814	94,947	96,867
	C	$25.00	1.000	60.0%	82,517	85,557	88,007	90,019	91,737	93,295
	D	$20.00	1.000	55.0%	83,857	85,469	86,943	88,252	89,429	90,515
	F	$15.00	1.000	50.0%	73,270	74,152	75,062	75,916	76,714	77,474
13 to 24		$10.00	1.000	46.0%	269,583	277,864	284,819	291,240	296,920	301,984
25 to 36		$6.00	1.000	42.0%	206,324	234,120	241,311	247,351	252,928	257,861
37 to 48		$4.00	1.000	38.0%	165,596	191,887	217,738	224,426	230,043	235,230
49 to 60		$3.00	1.000	34.0%	147,040	158,460	183,618	208,354	214,755	220,130
61+		$2.00	1.000	30.0%	600,763	734,635	877,587	1,042,836	1,229,637	1,419,837
Newbies	Free	$0.00	1.000	100.0%	43,611	43,611	43,611	43,611	43,611	43,611
	Paid	$20.00	1.000	0.0%	174,445	174,445	174,445	174,445	174,445	174,445

		Today	After Year 1	After Year 2	After Year 3	After Year 4	After Year 5
Merchandise Productivity			1.000	1.000	1.000	1.000	1.000
Profit Factor		40.0%	40.0%	40.0%	40.0%	40.0%	40.0%
New Names Free =		20.0%					
House Power =		0.500	After Year 1	After Year 2	After Year 3	After Year 4	After Year 5
Acquisition Power =		0.700					
Annual Demand		$88,376	$90,160	$92,425	$94,640	$96,682	$98,552
Annual Buyers		407,179	417,577	427,529	436,452	444,436	451,737
Marketing Cost		$20,271	$19,795	$20,714	$21,534	$22,279	$22,975
Variable Op. Profit		$15,079	$16,269	$16,256	$16,322	$16,393	$16,446
Profit % of Demand		17.1%	18.0%	17.6%	17.2%	17.0%	16.7%
Demand per Buyer		$217.04	$215.91	$216.18	$216.84	$217.54	$218.16
Cumm Demand			$90,160	$182,585	$277,225	$373,907	$472,459
Cumm Profit			$16,269	$32,524	$48,847	$65,240	$81,686

Here is the 40% spend level.

Lifetime Value and Customer Loyalty Worksheet

Author = Kevin Hillstrom, President, MineThatData

Recency	Grade	Mkt. $	Mkt. Chg.	Organic %	Today	After Year 1	After Year 2	After Year 3	After Year 4	After Year 5
0 to 12	A	$40.00	0.400	75.0%	83,747	84,170	85,949	88,015	90,031	91,909
	B	$32.00	1.000	67.0%	83,788	87,237	90,100	92,500	94,588	96,473
	C	$25.00	1.000	60.0%	82,517	85,554	88,025	90,036	91,747	93,297
	D	$20.00	1.000	55.0%	83,857	85,469	86,959	88,272	89,450	90,535
	F	$15.00	1.000	50.0%	73,270	74,152	75,070	75,926	76,726	77,486
13 to 24		$10.00	1.000	46.0%	269,583	278,860	285,381	291,650	297,235	302,234
25 to 36		$6.00	1.000	42.0%	206,324	234,120	242,176	247,839	253,284	258,134
37 to 48		$4.00	1.000	38.0%	165,596	191,887	217,738	225,230	230,497	235,561
49 to 60		$3.00	1.000	34.0%	147,040	158,460	183,618	208,354	215,524	220,564
61+		$2.00	1.000	30.0%	600,763	734,635	877,587	1,042,836	1,229,637	1,420,584
Newbies	Free	$0.00	1.000	100.0%	43,611	43,611	43,611	43,611	43,611	43,611
	Paid	$20.00	1.000	0.0%	174,445	174,445	174,445	174,445	174,445	174,445

			Merchandise Productivity			1.000	1.000	1.000	1.000	1.000
			Profit Factor		40.0%	40.0%	40.0%	40.0%	40.0%	40.0%
			New Names Free =		20.0%					
			House Power =		0.500	After	After	After	After	After
			Acquisition Power =		0.700	Year 1	Year 2	Year 3	Year 4	Year 5
			Annual Demand		$88,376	$89,616	$91,624	$93,692	$95,639	$97,442
			Annual Buyers		407,179	416,582	426,103	434,750	442,542	449,700
			Marketing Cost		$20,271	$19,460	$20,365	$21,169	$21,900	$22,582
			Variable Op. Profit		$15,079	$16,386	$16,284	$16,308	$16,356	$16,395
			Profit % of Demand		17.1%	18.3%	17.8%	17.4%	17.1%	16.8%
			Demand per Buyer		$217.04	$215.12	$215.03	$215.51	$216.11	$216.68
			Cumm Demand			$89,616	$181,240	$274,932	$370,571	$468,013
			Cumm Profit			$16,386	$32,670	$48,978	$65,334	$81,729

And the 30% spend level.

Lifetime Value and Customer Loyalty Worksheet

Author = Kevin Hillstrom, President, MineThatData

Recency	Grade	Mkt. $	Mkt. Chg.	Organic %	Today	After Year 1	After Year 2	After Year 3	After Year 4	After Year 5
0 to 12	A	$40.00	0.300	75.0%	83,747	83,241	84,591	86,423	88,293	90,069
	B	$32.00	1.000	67.0%	83,788	87,040	89,817	92,152	94,191	96,039
	C	$25.00	1.000	60.0%	82,517	85,551	88,044	90,055	91,759	93,298
	D	$20.00	1.000	55.0%	83,857	85,469	86,977	88,295	89,473	90,557
	F	$15.00	1.000	50.0%	73,270	74,152	75,080	75,938	76,739	77,499
13 to 24		$10.00	1.000	46.0%	269,583	279,989	285,995	292,091	297,571	302,501
25 to 36		$6.00	1.000	42.0%	206,324	234,120	243,157	248,373	253,667	258,425
37 to 48		$4.00	1.000	38.0%	165,596	191,887	217,738	226,143	230,993	235,917
49 to 60		$3.00	1.000	34.0%	147,040	158,460	183,618	208,354	216,397	221,039
61+		$2.00	1.000	30.0%	600,763	734,635	877,587	1,042,836	1,229,637	1,421,433
Newbies	Free	$0.00	1.000	100.0%	43,611	43,611	43,611	43,611	43,611	43,611
	Paid	$20.00	1.000	0.0%	174,445	174,445	174,445	174,445	174,445	174,445

			Merchandise Productivity			1.000	1.000	1.000	1.000	1.000
			Profit Factor		40.0%	40.0%	40.0%	40.0%	40.0%	40.0%
			New Names Free =		20.0%					
			House Power =		0.500	After Year 1	After Year 2	After Year 3	After Year 4	After Year 5
			Acquisition Power =		0.700					
			Annual Demand		$88,376	$88,999	$90,728	$92,641	$94,489	$96,222
			Annual Buyers		407,179	415,452	424,508	432,863	440,454	447,462
			Marketing Cost		$20,271	$19,125	$20,023	$20,813	$21,530	$22,199
			Variable Op. Profit		$15,079	$16,474	$16,268	$16,244	$16,266	$16,289
			Profit % of Demand		17.1%	18.5%	17.9%	17.5%	17.2%	16.9%
			Demand per Buyer		$217.04	$214.22	$213.72	$214.02	$214.53	$215.04
			Cumm Demand			$88,999	$179,727	$272,368	$366,857	$463,079
			Cumm Profit			$16,474	$32,743	$48,986	$65,252	$81,541

Look at cumm profit – it peaked at the 40% level, and got worse at the 30% level. Let's split the difference, and go with the 35% level.

Lifetime Value and Customer Loyalty Worksheet

Author = Kevin Hillstrom, President, MineThatData

Recency	Grade	Mkt. $	Mkt. Chg.	Organic %	Today	After Year 1	After Year 2	After Year 3	After Year 4	After Year 5
0 to 12	A	$40.00	0.350	75.0%	83,747	83,722	85,292	87,243	89,186	91,014
	B	$32.00	1.000	67.0%	83,788	87,142	89,963	92,331	94,395	96,262
	C	$25.00	1.000	60.0%	82,517	85,552	88,034	90,045	91,753	93,298
	D	$20.00	1.000	55.0%	83,857	85,469	86,967	88,283	89,461	90,546
	F	$15.00	1.000	50.0%	73,270	74,152	75,075	75,932	76,732	77,492
13 to 24		$10.00	1.000	46.0%	269,583	279,404	285,680	291,866	297,399	302,365
25 to 36		$6.00	1.000	42.0%	206,324	234,120	242,649	248,099	253,471	258,277
37 to 48		$4.00	1.000	38.0%	165,596	191,887	217,738	225,670	230,739	235,735
49 to 60		$3.00	1.000	34.0%	147,040	158,460	183,618	208,354	215,945	220,795
61+		$2.00	1.000	30.0%	600,763	734,635	877,587	1,042,836	1,229,637	1,420,994
Newbies	Free	$0.00	1.000	100.0%	43,611	43,611	43,611	43,611	43,611	43,611
	Paid	$20.00	1.000	0.0%	174,445	174,445	174,445	174,445	174,445	174,445

	Today	After Year 1	After Year 2	After Year 3	After Year 4	After Year 5
Merchandise Productivity		1.000	1.000	1.000	1.000	1.000
Profit Factor	40.0%	40.0%	40.0%	40.0%	40.0%	40.0%
New Names Free =	20.0%					
House Power =	0.500					
Acquisition Power =	0.700					

	Today	After Year 1	After Year 2	After Year 3	After Year 4	After Year 5
Annual Demand	$88,376	$89,319	$91,190	$93,183	$95,080	$96,848
Annual Buyers	407,179	416,037	425,331	433,835	441,528	448,611
Marketing Cost	$20,271	$19,293	$20,193	$20,990	$21,714	$22,389
Variable Op. Profit	$15,079	$16,435	$16,283	$16,283	$16,318	$16,350
Profit % of Demand	17.1%	18.4%	17.9%	17.5%	17.2%	16.9%
Demand per Buyer	$217.04	$214.69	$214.40	$214.79	$215.34	$215.89
Cumm Demand		$89,319	$180,509	$273,691	$368,771	$465,619
Cumm Profit		$16,435	$32,718	$49,001	$65,319	$81,669

The maximum level of profitability happened at about 40% of the current marketing spend.

	Base Case		Adjusted Case	
	Demand	Profit	Demand	Profit
Today	$88,376	$15,079	$88,376	$15,079
Year 1	$92,293	$15,447	$89,616	$16,386
Year 2	$95,670	$15,742	$91,624	$16,284
Year 3	$98,564	$15,967	$93,692	$16,308
Year 4	$101,060	$16,124	$95,639	$16,356
Year 5	$103,260	$16,228	$97,442	$16,395
Tot: Yr 1-5	$490,847	$79,508	$468,013	$81,729
Change			($22,834)	$2,221
Growth			-4.7%	2.8%

Look at Year 5. Top-line demand decreases from $103,260,000 to $97,442,000 ... it decreases by about six percent. However, profitability increases from $16,228,000 to $16,395,000. In total, over five years, we give up $22,834,000 of unprofitable demand in order to recoup $2,221,000 of profit.

This is part of a classic battle among Executives and Loyalty Marketers. If I were to present this story to 100 CEOs, it is likely that 80 of the 100 CEOs would not care about the $2.2 million in profit over five years. The 80 CEOs would argue that nearly $6,000,000 in market share is important, and they would be willing to sacrifice profit in an effort to maintain market share.

In other words, the "best practice" is to keep spending money to increase customer loyalty, even though shareholder value is compromised.

If the analysis is done for one high-level twelve-month buyer segment, it is easy to decide to maintain marketing spend "as-is".

What happens if we modify marketing spend for all existing buyer segments? Go ahead, play with the spreadsheet. Modify cells D6 – D15 until you maximize cumulative profit over the next five years. Take a few moments. I'll wait for you!

What did you learn?

Here is a scenario that I ran. Take a look.

Lifetime Value and Customer Loyalty Worksheet

Author = Kevin Hillstrom, President, MineThatData

Recency	Grade	Mkt. $	Mkt. Chg.	Organic %	Today	After Year 1	After Year 2	After Year 3	After Year 4	After Year 5
0 to 12	A	$40.00	0.400	75.0%	83,747	75,991	71,875	69,638	68,588	68,187
	B	$32.00	0.150	67.0%	83,788	72,644	71,016	70,447	70,353	70,478
	C	$25.00	0.050	60.0%	82,517	72,802	73,087	73,463	73,824	74,151
	D	$20.00	0.050	55.0%	83,857	78,519	79,299	79,832	80,263	80,630
	F	$15.00	0.050	50.0%	73,270	70,230	70,827	71,226	71,571	71,869
13 to 24		$10.00	0.250	46.0%	269,583	301,059	274,884	273,547	273,378	273,871
25 to 36		$6.00	0.150	42.0%	206,324	243,695	272,148	248,486	247,278	247,125
37 to 48		$4.00	0.150	38.0%	165,596	197,017	232,702	259,872	237,278	236,124
49 to 60		$3.00	0.100	34.0%	147,040	161,171	191,752	226,484	252,927	230,937
61+		$2.00	0.050	30.0%	600,763	741,415	895,011	1,077,663	1,293,256	1,533,402
Newbies	Free	$0.00	1.000	100.0%	43,611	43,611	43,611	43,611	43,611	43,611
	Paid	$20.00	1.000	0.0%	174,445	174,445	174,445	174,445	174,445	174,445

		Merchandise Productivity				1.000	1.000	1.000	1.000	1.000
		Profit Factor		40.0%	40.0%	40.0%	40.0%	40.0%	40.0%	40.0%
		New Names Free =		20.0%						
		House Power =		0.500	After Year 1	After Year 2	After Year 3	After Year 4	After Year 5	
		Acquisition Power =		0.700						
		Annual Demand			$88,376	$80,139	$77,529	$76,236	$75,703	$75,584
		Annual Buyers			407,179	370,186	366,103	364,607	364,599	365,315
		Marketing Cost			$20,271	$7,408	$7,361	$7,295	$7,278	$7,276
		Variable Op. Profit			$15,079	$24,647	$23,651	$23,200	$23,004	$22,958
		Profit % of Demand			17.1%	30.8%	30.5%	30.4%	30.4%	30.4%
		Demand per Buyer			$217.04	$216.48	$211.77	$209.09	$207.63	$206.90
		Cumm Demand				$80,139	$157,668	$233,904	$309,608	$385,192
		Cumm Profit				$24,647	$48,298	$71,498	$94,502	$117,460

I mean, this business is spending embarrassing amounts of money marketing to existing customers, don't you think? Look at annual marketing expense – it drops from $20.3 million per year down to $7.4 million per year. We reduce marketing spend by sixty-five percent – that's a huge number – huge! HUGE!

Now look at the comparison between annual demand and annual profit.

	Base Case		Adjusted Case	
	Demand	Profit	Demand	Profit
Today	$88,376	$15,079	$88,376	$15,079
Year 1	$92,293	$15,447	$80,139	$24,647
Year 2	$95,670	$15,742	$77,529	$23,651
Year 3	$98,564	$15,967	$76,236	$23,200
Year 4	$101,060	$16,124	$75,703	$23,004
Year 5	$103,260	$16,228	$75,584	$22,958
Tot: Yr 1-5	$490,847	$79,508	$385,192	$117,460
Change			($105,655)	$37,952
Growth			-21.5%	47.7%

By year five, the business has shrunk, from $103 million down to $76 million. That's a much smaller business. But in year five, profit increases from $16.2 million to $23.0 million. Across the five year timeframe, demand shrinks by 22%, profit increases by 48%.

Let's pretend that you are the CEO. Would you be willing to stomach a drop in top-line demand over a five year period of time? Would you be willing to lead a business that is this much smaller?

Think about this carefully. Over five years, you return nearly $38 million in profit to shareholders/owners. The business is significantly healthier. But the business is smaller.

If I polled 100 CEOs, it is very likely that 80 CEOs would demand that we operate business "as-is". It is very likely that the drop in top-line demand would be too severe to stomach.

And that's what is wrong with loyalty marketing, and business in general. Wins and losses should be measured in terms of profit (and cash). Think about it this way. Say you earned $100,000 a year for your salary. However, after taxes, you took home $55,000, and your annual expenses of $50,000 left you with $5,000 in savings. Are you in better shape than another individual who earned $70,000 a year for a salary, took home $42,000 after taxes, and had $32,000 in annual expenses, saving $10,000?

No, you are not in better shape. The individual earning a lower salary is in better shape, because she manages her expenses better, leaving her with more cash at the end of the year. We would all agree she did a better job of managing cash during the year.

But in business, we reward the individual who earns a higher salary.

Enough preaching.

There are ways to fight back.

To date, the entire argument has been centered on customer loyalty. We demonstrated that we are spending too much money marketing to existing customers, and that money is not being spent profitably. But what happens if we spend more money on customer acquisition activities? Are customer acquisition activities being managed optimally?

Let's go back to the optimized case.

Lifetime Value and Customer Loyalty Worksheet

Author = Kevin Hillstrom, President, MineThatData

Recency	Grade	Mkt. $	Mkt. Chg.	Organic %	Today	After Year 1	After Year 2	After Year 3	After Year 4	After Year 5
0 to 12	A	$40.00	0.400	75.0%	83,747	75,991	71,875	69,638	68,588	68,187
	B	$32.00	0.150	67.0%	83,788	72,644	71,016	70,447	70,353	70,478
	C	$25.00	0.050	60.0%	82,517	72,802	73,087	73,463	73,824	74,151
	D	$20.00	0.050	55.0%	83,857	78,519	79,299	79,832	80,263	80,630
	F	$15.00	0.050	50.0%	73,270	70,230	70,827	71,226	71,571	71,869
13 to 24		$10.00	0.250	46.0%	269,583	301,059	274,884	273,547	273,378	273,871
25 to 36		$6.00	0.150	42.0%	206,324	243,695	272,148	248,486	247,278	247,125
37 to 48		$4.00	0.150	38.0%	165,596	197,017	232,702	259,872	237,278	236,124
49 to 60		$3.00	0.100	34.0%	147,040	161,171	191,752	226,484	252,927	230,937
61+		$2.00	0.050	30.0%	600,763	741,415	895,011	1,077,663	1,293,256	1,533,402
Newbies	Free	$0.00	1.000	100.0%	43,611	43,611	43,611	43,611	43,611	43,611
	Paid	$20.00	1.000	0.0%	174,445	174,445	174,445	174,445	174,445	174,445

		Merchandise Productivity				1.000	1.000	1.000	1.000	1.000
		Profit Factor			40.0%	40.0%	40.0%	40.0%	40.0%	40.0%
		New Names Free =			20.0%					
		House Power =			0.500	After Year 1	After Year 2	After Year 3	After Year 4	After Year 5
		Acquisition Power =			0.700					
		Annual Demand			$88,376	$80,139	$77,529	$76,236	$75,703	$75,584
		Annual Buyers			407,179	370,186	366,103	364,607	364,599	365,315
		Marketing Cost			$20,271	$7,408	$7,361	$7,295	$7,278	$7,276
		Variable Op. Profit			$15,079	$24,647	$23,651	$23,200	$23,004	$22,958
		Profit % of Demand			17.1%	30.8%	30.5%	30.4%	30.4%	30.4%
		Demand per Buyer			$217.04	$216.48	$211.77	$209.09	$207.63	$206.90
		Cumm Demand				$80,139	$157,668	$233,904	$309,608	$385,192
		Cumm Profit				$24,647	$48,298	$71,498	$94,502	$117,460

Look at cell D17. We can change this cell, to see what happens to the business when we increase customer acquisition spend.

Let's change cell D17 from 1.00 to 1.10. We will spend 10% more trying to acquire more customers.

Lifetime Value and Customer Loyalty Worksheet

Author = Kevin Hillstrom, President, MineThatData

Recency	Grade	Mkt. $	Mkt. Chg.	Organic %	Today	After Year 1	After Year 2	After Year 3	After Year 4	After Year 5
0 to 12	A	$40.00	0.400	75.0%	83,747	76,796	73,366	71,764	71,180	71,104
	B	$32.00	0.150	67.0%	83,788	74,162	73,191	73,156	73,402	73,755
	C	$25.00	0.050	60.0%	82,517	75,323	76,069	76,766	77,335	77,811
	D	$20.00	0.050	55.0%	83,857	82,178	83,153	83,820	84,348	84,793
	F	$15.00	0.050	50.0%	73,270	73,764	74,449	74,911	75,305	75,646
13 to 24		$10.00	0.250	46.0%	269,583	301,059	284,830	284,852	285,744	286,962
25 to 36		$6.00	0.150	42.0%	206,324	243,695	272,148	257,477	257,497	258,304
37 to 48		$4.00	0.150	38.0%	165,596	197,017	232,702	259,872	245,863	245,883
49 to 60		$3.00	0.100	34.0%	147,040	161,171	191,752	226,484	252,927	239,293
61+		$2.00	0.050	30.0%	600,763	741,415	895,011	1,077,663	1,293,256	1,533,402
Newbies	Free	$0.00	1.000	100.0%	43,611	43,611	43,611	43,611	43,611	43,611
	Paid	$20.00	1.100	0.0%	174,445	186,480	186,480	186,480	186,480	186,480

			Merchandise Productivity			1.000	1.000	1.000	1.000	1.000
			Profit Factor		40.0%	40.0%	40.0%	40.0%	40.0%	40.0%
			New Names Free =		20.0%					
			House Power =		0.500	After	After	After	After	After
			Acquisition Power =		0.700	Year 1	Year 2	Year 3	Year 4	Year 5
			Annual Demand		$88,376	$81,856	$79,841	$79,060	$78,900	$79,044
			Annual Buyers		407,179	382,222	380,228	380,417	381,570	383,109
			Marketing Cost		$20,271	$8,175	$8,157	$8,131	$8,139	$8,156
			Variable Op. Profit		$15,079	$24,567	$23,779	$23,493	$23,421	$23,462
			Profit % of Demand		17.1%	30.0%	29.8%	29.7%	29.7%	29.7%
			Demand per Buyer		$217.04	$214.16	$209.98	$207.82	$206.78	$206.32
			Cumm Demand			$81,856	$161,697	$240,757	$319,656	$398,700
			Cumm Profit			$24,567	$48,346	$71,839	$95,260	$118,721

Oh my goodness. Top-line demand begins to grow again, marketing expense grows marginally, and profit improves. Turns out we are under-investing in customer acquisition.

Change cell D17 to 1.20.

Lifetime Value and Customer Loyalty Worksheet

Author = Kevin Hillstrom, President, MineThatData

Recency	Grade	Mkt. $	Mkt. Chg.	Organic %	Today	After Year 1	After Year 2	After Year 3	After Year 4	After Year 5
0 to 12	A	$40.00	0.400	75.0%	83,747	77,579	74,816	73,833	73,701	73,943
	B	$32.00	0.150	67.0%	83,788	75,639	75,307	75,791	76,369	76,944
	C	$25.00	0.050	60.0%	82,517	77,776	78,971	79,980	80,752	81,372
	D	$20.00	0.050	55.0%	83,857	85,738	86,904	87,700	88,324	88,843
	F	$15.00	0.050	50.0%	73,270	77,202	77,974	78,498	78,938	79,321
13 to 24		$10.00	0.250	46.0%	269,583	301,059	294,508	295,853	297,777	299,700
25 to 36		$6.00	0.150	42.0%	206,324	243,695	272,148	266,226	267,442	269,182
37 to 48		$4.00	0.150	38.0%	165,596	197,017	232,702	259,872	254,217	255,378
49 to 60		$3.00	0.100	34.0%	147,040	161,171	191,752	226,484	252,927	247,424
61+		$2.00	0.050	30.0%	600,763	741,415	895,011	1,077,663	1,293,256	1,533,402
Newbies	Free	$0.00	1.000	100.0%	43,611	43,611	43,611	43,611	43,611	43,611
	Paid	$20.00	1.200	0.0%	174,445	198,191	198,191	198,191	198,191	198,191

			Merchandise Productivity			1.000	1.000	1.000	1.000	1.000
			Profit Factor		40.0%	40.0%	40.0%	40.0%	40.0%	40.0%
			New Names Free =		20.0%					
			House Power =		0.500	After Year 1	After Year 2	After Year 3	After Year 4	After Year 5
			Acquisition Power =		0.700					
			Annual Demand		$88,376	$83,526	$82,091	$81,807	$82,010	$82,410
			Annual Buyers		407,179	393,933	393,973	395,801	398,084	400,423
			Marketing Cost		$20,271	$8,993	$9,004	$9,016	$9,048	$9,083
			Variable Op. Profit		$15,079	$24,417	$23,833	$23,707	$23,756	$23,881
			Profit % of Demand		17.1%	29.2%	29.0%	29.0%	29.0%	29.0%
			Demand per Buyer		$217.04	$212.03	$208.37	$206.69	$206.01	$205.81
			Cumm Demand			$83,526	$165,617	$247,424	$329,434	$411,844
			Cumm Profit			$24,417	$48,250	$71,957	$95,712	$119,594

The business is even more profitable. Top-line sales improve again.

Change cell D17 to 1.30.

58

Lifetime Value and Customer Loyalty Worksheet

Author = Kevin Hillstrom, President, MineThatData

Recency	Grade	Mkt. $	Mkt. Chg.	Organic %	Today	After Year 1	After Year 2	After Year 3	After Year 4	After Year 5
0 to 12	A	$40.00	0.400	75.0%	83,747	78,342	76,231	75,850	76,161	76,712
	B	$32.00	0.150	67.0%	83,788	77,080	77,371	78,361	79,263	80,053
	C	$25.00	0.050	60.0%	82,517	80,169	81,800	83,114	84,083	84,846
	D	$20.00	0.050	55.0%	83,857	89,209	90,562	91,485	92,201	92,794
	F	$15.00	0.050	50.0%	73,270	80,555	81,412	81,995	82,481	82,905
13 to 24		$10.00	0.250	46.0%	269,583	301,059	303,946	306,581	309,513	312,123
25 to 36		$6.00	0.150	42.0%	206,324	243,695	272,148	274,758	277,140	279,790
37 to 48		$4.00	0.150	38.0%	165,596	197,017	232,702	259,872	262,365	264,639
49 to 60		$3.00	0.100	34.0%	147,040	161,171	191,752	226,484	252,927	255,353
61+		$2.00	0.050	30.0%	600,763	741,415	895,011	1,077,663	1,293,256	1,533,402
Newbies	Free	$0.00	1.000	100.0%	43,611	43,611	43,611	43,611	43,611	43,611
	Paid	$20.00	1.300	0.0%	174,445	209,613	209,613	209,613	209,613	209,613

		Merchandise Productivity				1.000	1.000	1.000	1.000	1.000
		Profit Factor		40.0%		40.0%	40.0%	40.0%	40.0%	40.0%
		New Names Free =		20.0%						
		House Power =		0.500		After Year 1	After Year 2	After Year 3	After Year 4	After Year 5
		Acquisition Power =		0.700						
		Annual Demand			$88,376	$85,154	$84,285	$84,487	$85,043	$85,693
		Annual Buyers			407,179	405,355	407,377	410,805	414,189	417,309
		Marketing Cost			$20,271	$9,860	$9,898	$9,949	$10,004	$10,056
		Variable Op. Profit			$15,079	$24,202	$23,816	$23,846	$24,013	$24,221
		Profit % of Demand			17.1%	28.4%	28.3%	28.2%	28.2%	28.3%
		Demand per Buyer			$217.04	$210.07	$206.90	$205.66	$205.32	$205.35
		Cumm Demand				$85,154	$169,440	$253,927	$338,970	$424,663
		Cumm Profit				$24,202	$48,018	$71,864	$95,877	$120,097

Five-year profit improves again. We are significantly under-spending on customer acquisition.

Let's ramp up customer acquisition spend to 1.40.

Lifetime Value and Customer Loyalty Worksheet

Author = Kevin Hillstrom, President, MineThatData

Recency	Grade	Mkt. $	Mkt. Chg.	Organic %	Today	After Year 1	After Year 2	After Year 3	After Year 4	After Year 5
0 to 12	A	$40.00	0.400	75.0%	83,747	79,088	77,614	77,822	78,564	79,417
	B	$32.00	0.150	67.0%	83,788	78,487	79,388	80,873	82,090	83,092
	C	$25.00	0.050	60.0%	82,517	82,507	84,566	86,177	87,339	88,240
	D	$20.00	0.050	55.0%	83,857	92,602	94,136	95,183	95,989	96,654
	F	$15.00	0.050	50.0%	73,270	83,831	84,772	85,413	85,944	86,407
13 to 24		$10.00	0.250	46.0%	269,583	301,059	313,169	317,065	320,981	324,262
25 to 36		$6.00	0.150	42.0%	206,324	243,695	272,148	283,096	286,617	290,157
37 to 48		$4.00	0.150	38.0%	165,596	197,017	232,702	259,872	270,326	273,689
49 to 60		$3.00	0.100	34.0%	147,040	161,171	191,752	226,484	252,927	263,102
61+		$2.00	0.050	30.0%	600,763	741,415	895,011	1,077,663	1,293,256	1,533,402
Newbies	Free	$0.00	1.000	100.0%	43,611	43,611	43,611	43,611	43,611	43,611
	Paid	$20.00	1.400	0.0%	174,445	220,774	220,774	220,774	220,774	220,774

	Today	After Year 1	After Year 2	After Year 3	After Year 4	After Year 5
Merchandise Productivity		1.000	1.000	1.000	1.000	1.000
Profit Factor	40.0%	40.0%	40.0%	40.0%	40.0%	40.0%
New Names Free =	20.0%					
House Power =	0.500	After Year 1	After Year 2	After Year 3	After Year 4	After Year 5
Acquisition Power =	0.700					
Annual Demand	$88,376	$86,746	$86,430	$87,105	$88,007	$88,901
Annual Buyers	407,179	416,516	420,476	425,467	429,927	433,810
Marketing Cost	$20,271	$10,774	$10,841	$10,928	$11,006	$11,076
Variable Op. Profit	$15,079	$23,924	$23,731	$23,914	$24,196	$24,485
Profit % of Demand	17.1%	27.6%	27.5%	27.5%	27.5%	27.5%
Demand per Buyer	$217.04	$208.27	$205.55	$204.73	$204.70	$204.93
Cumm Demand		$86,746	$173,175	$260,281	$348,288	$437,189
Cumm Profit		$23,924	$47,655	$71,570	$95,766	$120,251

Well, we are closing in on the optimal solution, aren't we? If I type in 1.45 or 1.50, I find that five-year profit begins to decline.

I cut my investments in loyal buyers, dramatically. Then, I invest more money acquiring first-time buyers. Here's the net of the relationship.

	Base Case		Adjusted Case	
	Demand	Profit	Demand	Profit
Today	$88,376	$15,079	$88,376	$15,079
Year 1	$92,293	$15,447	$86,746	$23,924
Year 2	$95,670	$15,742	$86,430	$23,731
Year 3	$98,564	$15,967	$87,105	$23,914
Year 4	$101,060	$16,124	$88,007	$24,196
Year 5	$103,260	$16,228	$88,901	$24,485
Tot: Yr 1-5	$490,847	$79,508	$437,189	$120,251
Change			($53,658)	$40,743
Growth			-10.9%	51.2%

Top-line demand has flattened out, but profit is dramatically improved. In year five, demand is down by fourteen million, but profit increases by eight million. For the five year period in total, demand drops by fifty-four million, but profit increases by forty-one million.

Can you see how badly this business was being mis-managed?

And yet, 80 out of 100 CEOs would look at this scenario, and they would shake their heads. "We're not growing ... WE'RE NOT GROWING!"

Fine. I'll go back in and invest more money on existing buyers. Let's change cells D6 – D15 from their optimized levels to a level of 0.60 for each cell. We'll try to appease our CEO. What happens?

Lifetime Value and Customer Loyalty Worksheet

Author = Kevin Hillstrom, President, MineThatData

Recency	Grade	Mkt. $	Mkt. Chg.	Organic %	Today	After Year 1	After Year 2	After Year 3	After Year 4	After Year 5
0 to 12	A	$40.00	0.600	75.0%	83,747	85,822	89,055	92,772	96,122	98,973
	B	$32.00	0.600	67.0%	83,788	88,210	92,556	96,462	99,539	102,047
	C	$25.00	0.600	60.0%	82,517	90,884	94,802	97,767	100,078	102,010
	D	$20.00	0.600	55.0%	83,857	97,210	99,467	101,150	102,581	103,842
	F	$15.00	0.600	50.0%	73,270	86,441	87,743	88,746	89,648	90,490
13 to 24		$10.00	0.600	46.0%	269,583	283,961	316,978	326,969	335,409	342,398
25 to 36		$6.00	0.600	42.0%	206,324	238,436	251,153	280,355	289,192	296,657
37 to 48		$4.00	0.600	38.0%	165,596	193,774	223,933	235,877	263,302	271,602
49 to 60		$3.00	0.600	34.0%	147,040	159,457	186,591	215,632	227,132	253,541
61+		$2.00	0.600	30.0%	600,763	736,676	882,982	1,053,918	1,251,031	1,456,864
Newbies	Free	$0.00	1.000	100.0%	43,611	43,611	43,611	43,611	43,611	43,611
	Paid	$20.00	1.400	0.0%	174,445	220,774	220,774	220,774	220,774	220,774

Merchandise Productivity		1.000	1.000	1.000	1.000	1.000
Profit Factor	40.0%	40.0%	40.0%	40.0%	40.0%	40.0%
New Names Free =	20.0%					
House Power =	0.500	After	After	After	After	After
Acquisition Power =	0.700	Year 1	Year 2	Year 3	Year 4	Year 5
Annual Demand	$88,376	$93,889	$97,296	$100,717	$103,724	$106,288
Annual Buyers	407,179	448,567	463,622	476,897	487,968	497,361
Marketing Cost	$20,271	$17,992	$18,986	$19,786	$20,475	$21,080
Variable Op. Profit	$15,079	$19,563	$19,932	$20,501	$21,015	$21,436
Profit % of Demand	17.1%	20.8%	20.5%	20.4%	20.3%	20.2%
Demand per Buyer	$217.04	$209.31	$209.86	$211.19	$212.56	$213.70
Cumm Demand		$93,889	$191,184	$291,901	$395,626	$501,914
Cumm Profit		$19,563	$39,495	$59,996	$81,011	$102,446

Isn't that scenario interesting?

Here's the net comparison against our base case.

	Base Case		Adjusted Case	
	Demand	Profit	Demand	Profit
Today	$88,376	$15,079	$88,376	$15,079
Year 1	$92,293	$15,447	$93,889	$19,563
Year 2	$95,670	$15,742	$97,296	$19,932
Year 3	$98,564	$15,967	$100,717	$20,501
Year 4	$101,060	$16,124	$103,724	$21,015
Year 5	$103,260	$16,228	$106,288	$21,436
Tot: Yr 1-5	$490,847	$79,508	$501,914	$102,446
Change			$11,067	$22,938
Growth			2.3%	28.9%

There we go – our CEO could hardly argue with this scenario, right?

Demand increases by $11,000,000 over the five year period of time.

Profit increases by $23,000,000 over the five year period of time.

Marketing expenses are reduced by about 10% per year.

What is not to like about this scenario?

What is the lesson of this simulation exercise (and believe me, there has to be a lesson, or why waste your time and money)?

While this exercise was purposely exaggerated to make a point, the story is consistent across my client base. We continually spend too much money marketing to existing buyers, in an effort to drive customer loyalty. We continually de-emphasize spend in customer acquisition efforts, believing that it is more effective to retain an existing customer than it is to acquire a new customer. Oh yes, we hear countless derivations of that sentence, don't we? How many people, in your opinion, have run the simulation exercise we just ran? How many validate the hypothesis? Just how many people confirm whether conventional wisdom is right or not?

In the vast majority of my simulations, this is how the story turns out. The story is very likely to turn out this way if the brand retains fewer than 40% of last year's twelve-month buyer file. In those situations, the long-term value gained by increasing investment to existing buyers is usually so bad that the long-term value of a new customer exceeds it.

Allow me to repeat the sentence, because the entire booklet has been leading up to this sentence:

"The long-term value gained by increasing investment to existing buyers is usually so bad that the long-term value of a new customer exceeds it."

Remember, if you are working at Starbucks, or Amazon, or Wal-Mart, or Target, or McDonalds, or any other business where customers shop daily or weekly or monthly, then these rules do not apply to you.

But if you work at most e-commerce, retail, and/or catalog brands, where annual repurchase rates are under 40%, then the simulation I just shared with you in this booklet replicates nicely. It is very likely that you should spend less on loyalty marketing initiatives, simply because too few customers will ever become loyal. Your investments do not bear fruit. However, investments in customer acquisition programs do bear fruit.

Merchandise Productivity

Here's a secret that few marketers understand, but most marketers should embrace. Ready?

"*When merchandise productivity increases, customers become more loyal, and marketers can afford to profitably spend more money marketing to loyal buyers*."

Name one loyalty marketer that doesn't like hearing that sentence?

"Merchandise Productivity" is simply defined as *selling merchandise that customers like more than the merchandise previously sold*. The secret to business is embedded within merchandise productivity. When your merchandising team finds items that customers like better this year than last year, sales grow, and more important for marketers, marketing effectiveness looks much better, allowing the marketer to spend more. As you know, marketers love the opportunity to spend more!

Here's the scenario we sold to our CEO:

Lifetime Value and Customer Loyalty Worksheet

Author = Kevin Hillstrom, President, MineThatData

Recency	Grade	Mkt. $	Mkt. Chg.	Organic %	Today	After Year 1	After Year 2	After Year 3	After Year 4	After Year 5
0 to 12	A	$40.00	0.600	75.0%	83,747	85,822	89,055	92,772	96,122	98,973
	B	$32.00	0.600	67.0%	83,788	88,210	92,556	96,462	99,539	102,047
	C	$25.00	0.600	60.0%	82,517	90,884	94,802	97,767	100,078	102,010
	D	$20.00	0.600	55.0%	83,857	97,210	99,467	101,150	102,581	103,842
	F	$15.00	0.600	50.0%	73,270	86,441	87,743	88,746	89,648	90,490
13 to 24		$10.00	0.600	46.0%	269,583	283,961	316,978	326,969	335,409	342,398
25 to 36		$6.00	0.600	42.0%	206,324	238,436	251,153	280,355	289,192	296,657
37 to 48		$4.00	0.600	38.0%	165,596	193,774	223,933	235,877	263,302	271,602
49 to 60		$3.00	0.600	34.0%	147,040	159,457	186,591	215,632	227,132	253,541
61+		$2.00	0.600	30.0%	600,763	736,676	882,982	1,053,918	1,251,031	1,456,864
Newbies	Free	$0.00	1.000	100.0%	43,611	43,611	43,611	43,611	43,611	43,611
	Paid	$20.00	1.400	0.0%	174,445	220,774	220,774	220,774	220,774	220,774

			Merchandise Productivity			1.000	1.000	1.000	1.000	1.000
			Profit Factor		40.0%	40.0%	40.0%	40.0%	40.0%	40.0%
			New Names Free =		20.0%					
			House Power =		0.500	After Year 1	After Year 2	After Year 3	After Year 4	After Year 5
			Acquisition Power =		0.700					
			Annual Demand		$88,376	$93,889	$97,296	$100,717	$103,724	$106,288
			Annual Buyers		407,179	448,567	463,622	476,897	487,968	497,361
			Marketing Cost		$20,271	$17,992	$18,986	$19,786	$20,475	$21,080
			Variable Op. Profit		$15,079	$19,563	$19,932	$20,501	$21,015	$21,436
			Profit % of Demand		17.1%	20.8%	20.5%	20.4%	20.3%	20.2%
			Demand per Buyer		$217.04	$209.31	$209.86	$211.19	$212.56	$213.70
			Cumm Demand			$93,889	$191,184	$291,901	$395,626	$501,914
			Cumm Profit			$19,563	$39,495	$59,996	$81,011	$102,446

Now, let's assume that merchandise productivity increases by 10% - in other words, let's pretend that customers love the merchandise offered by our business so much that they spend 10% more. Here's what the business looks like:

Lifetime Value and Customer Loyalty Worksheet

Author = Kevin Hillstrom, President, MineThatData

Recency	Grade	Mkt. $	Mkt. Chg.	Organic %	Today	After Year 1	After Year 2	After Year 3	After Year 4	After Year 5
0 to 12	A	$40.00	0.600	75.0%	83,747	94,404	104,102	113,143	120,667	126,770
	B	$32.00	0.600	67.0%	83,788	97,032	105,613	112,825	118,372	122,781
	C	$25.00	0.600	60.0%	82,517	99,972	106,139	110,679	114,202	117,135
	D	$20.00	0.600	55.0%	83,857	106,930	110,007	112,257	114,188	115,892
	F	$15.00	0.600	50.0%	73,270	95,085	96,742	98,003	99,147	100,223
13 to 24		$10.00	0.600	46.0%	269,583	271,639	334,200	350,943	364,450	375,376
25 to 36		$6.00	0.600	42.0%	206,324	235,321	237,117	291,727	306,341	318,132
37 to 48		$4.00	0.600	38.0%	165,596	192,519	219,577	221,252	272,208	285,845
49 to 60		$3.00	0.600	34.0%	147,040	158,843	184,669	210,623	212,229	261,108
61+		$2.00	0.600	30.0%	600,763	735,563	879,972	1,047,512	1,237,985	1,427,355
Newbies	Free	$0.00	1.000	100.0%	43,611	47,972	47,972	47,972	47,972	47,972
	Paid	$20.00	1.400	0.0%	174,445	242,851	242,851	242,851	242,851	242,851

					After Year 1	After Year 2	After Year 3	After Year 4	After Year 5
Merchandise Productivity					1.100	1.100	1.100	1.100	1.100
Profit Factor		40.0%			40.0%	40.0%	40.0%	40.0%	40.0%
New Names Free =		20.0%							
House Power =		0.500							
Acquisition Power =		0.700							

	Today	After Year 1	After Year 2	After Year 3	After Year 4	After Year 5
Annual Demand	$88,376	$103,277	$111,674	$119,073	$125,220	$130,250
Annual Buyers	407,179	493,424	522,602	546,908	566,576	582,801
Marketing Cost	$20,271	$18,765	$20,375	$21,583	$22,594	$23,455
Variable Op. Profit	$15,079	$22,546	$24,295	$26,046	$27,494	$28,645
Profit % of Demand	17.1%	21.8%	21.8%	21.9%	22.0%	22.0%
Demand per Buyer	$217.04	$209.31	$213.69	$217.72	$221.01	$223.49
Cumm Demand		$103,277	$214,951	$334,024	$459,244	$589,494
Cumm Profit		$22,546	$46,841	$72,887	$100,381	$129,027

Cumm profit increases from $102 million to $129 million, growing by nearly 30% because of the 10% increase in merchandise productivity.

Let that fact sink in for a moment … profit increased by nearly 30% because of a 10% increase in merchandise productivity.

Why wouldn't all of our efforts be focused on helping the merchandising team figure out the merchandise that resonates most with the target customer audience?

That's where our efforts should be spent, if we want to increase customer loyalty. Instead, we largely ignore the merchandising team, suggesting that they are "*difficult to work with*". We instead hope to "*engage*" a customer via a 140 character tweet, thinking that will more than make up for a broken relationship with the merchandising team.

Help your merchandising team! Why? Because you get to spend more on marketing activities. If your business is close to optimized, then a 10% increase in merchandise productivity gives you the ability to spend marketing dollars profitably.

Honestly, the secret to business is aligning merchandise with customers. In retail, stores are customized by market, in an effort to grow comp store sales. That is the essence of increasing merchandise productivity.

In e-commerce, the largest brands personalize every single home page and landing page the customer sees. Merchandise is tailored to the customer based on what the customer previously purchased, what the customer previously viewed online, and where else the customer visits online. It is common to see 20% productivity gains – I just had a client tell me they saw a 50% productivity gain by personalizing just the home page and key landing pages. This allows that client to spend a fortune on marketing, because the marketing dollars are overwhelmingly profitable. Better yet, merchandise productivity gains lead to increased customer loyalty, and we all want loyal customers, don't we?

What Did We Learn?

The point of this booklet is to flip the narrative on customer loyalty.

For the vast majority of businesses we work for, customers are not loyal. Customers have a need at a point in time, and we solve that need, hopefully profitably. From that point forward, a minority of customers purchase for a second time. We can increase the odds of a customer purchasing for a second time, but we cannot force the customer to become loyal.

For most of the businesses we manage, maybe three in one hundred customers achieve loyal status. The rest of the customers ultimately churn. We literally re-invent our customer base every three to five years. If we cannot generate profit from the transactions that customers place, we cannot ever hope to have a healthy business.

Unfortunately, we are largely seduced by the thought that a marketing program can cause customers to become loyal. We all think about our own personal habits … gamely trying to roll past 25,000 miles traveled on an annual basis so that we earn the perk of being able to sit in a seat with three additional inches of leg room. We fly ten times a year to achieve this heroic state of mind, only to learn that we're not really earning financial rewards but instead are earning emotional rewards. We spend a fortune, but are not rewarded commensurately. Then, we think we can apply the same logic to our business. Even though customers only buy widgets two times per year, we think we can inspire loyal behavior. We throw discounts and promotions and freebies and points at the customer, doing everything possible to push the customer from two widget purchases per year to six widget purchases per year. Instead, we push the customer to 2.2 widget purchases per year. The top-line doesn't move, and worse, the bottom-line falters. We spend marketing dollars that do not generate profit.

In the vast majority of client projects, when the annual repurchase rate for the twelve-month buyer file is under 40%, I am able to demonstrate via a spreadsheet simulation that marketing is investing too much money on existing buyers. Marketing would be better served to cut back on spend among existing buyers, focusing instead on spending an appropriate level of money to acquire new customers. This trend repeats all the time, or I wouldn't bother to share the fact with you.

The thing that does move the loyalty needle, to some extent, is merchandise productivity. When customers love the merchandise we sell, customers become more loyal. When customers become more loyal, it is common that we can spend more money on marketing activities, further accelerating customer loyalty. But it all starts with merchandise productivity. In the vast majority of cases, marketers literally ignore merchandise productivity. This is the first place where marketers should spend time. Marketers need to identify the merchandise that customers love the most. Marketers need to identify the new merchandise that customers seem to like, and then promote those items. If marketers personalized the home page, landing pages, and email campaigns across existing customers, merchandise productivity would increase by 20% +/- and the corresponding gain in merchandise productivity would fund loyalty initiatives while increasing company profitability. The marketer would look good. The company profit and loss statement would look good. The customer would feel good.

We can increase customer loyalty. But our focus is wrong. We need to avoid gimmicks and promotions. We need to focus on the merchandise that customers love.

If we have to manage customer loyalty, focus on customers who have a 60% chance of purchasing again in the next twelve months. Among that audience, try hard to find low-cost emotional benefits that can grow sales. Think about the Nordstrom Anniversary Sale example I offered earlier in the booklet. Because it is terribly hard to increase customer spend (loyalty) by more than 15% via marketing programs, we tend to generate sales but lose money in the process. Nobody wins when the customer spends more but the company earns less.

If your company possesses a twelve-month buyer file with an annual repurchase rate under 40%, focus your efforts on merchandise productivity via personalization and on low-cost customer acquisition.

If your company possesses a twelve-month buyer file with an annual repurchase rate over 60%, you have a shot at making profit via loyalty initiatives. Try hard to minimize the expenses associated with your loyalty program.

If you are Starbucks, Wal-Mart, Target, or Amazon, you have free reign to try what you want – have at it!!!

www.ingramcontent.com/pod-product-compliance
Lightning Source LLC
Chambersburg PA
CBHW040840180526
45159CB00001B/255